John Watts De Peyster

Secession in Switzerland and in the United States compared

John Watts De Peyster

Secession in Switzerland and in the United States compared

ISBN/EAN: 9783337153748

Printed in Europe, USA, Canada, Australia, Japan

Cover: Foto ©ninafisch / pixelio.de

More available books at **www.hansebooks.com**

Secession in Switzerland

AND IN THE

UNITED STATES

COMPARED:

BEING THE

ANNUAL ADDRESS,

DELIVERED OCT. 20TH, 1863, BEFORE THE

Vermont State Historical Society,

IN THE

HALL OF REPRESENTATIVES,

CAPITOL,

MONTPELIER,

BY

J. WATTS DE PEYSTER.

" Do Thou direct Thy Chariot, Lord,
  And guide it at Thy will ;
Without Thy aid our Strength is vain,
  And useless all our Skill."

"Send down Thy Peace and banish Strife,
  Let Bitterness depart ;
Revive the Spirit of the Past
  In every Switzer's heart."
        ZWINGLI, THE SWISS REFORMER'S HYMN.

CATSKILL
JOSEPH JOESBURY, PRINTER, "JOURNAL OFFICE."
1863.

SECESSION IN SWITZERLAND.

"The drum was beat; and. lo!
The plough. the workshop is forsaken, all
Swarm to the old familiar long loved banners."

"What? shall this 'land' become a field of slaughter,
And brother-killing Discord, fire-eyed,
Be let loose through its 'vales' to roam and rage?
Shall the decision be deliver'd over
To deaf remorseless Rage, that bears no leader?
Here is not room for battle, only for butchery.
Well, let it be! I have long thought of it,
So let it burst then!"

SCHILLER'S DEATH OF WALLENSTEIN.

History is the School of Princes. It is their duty to derive Instruction therefrom in regard to the Errors of Times Past, in order to avoid them; to understand that they must form for themselves a System; to learn to follow that out step by step; and to know that the Ruler, who has calculated his course of conduct the most wisely, is the only one who can get the better of those who act less in accordance with the lesson than he.

FREDERIC THE GREAT.

The History of Foreign Nations is only interesting to us on account of its relations (analogies) with our own, or of the great achievements, whose performance is recorded therein.

VOLTAIRE.

A student of history, not satisfied with mere superficial examination but ever urged to a closer and closer comparison of analogies, I have often been struck with the perspicuity of every sentiment of Jewry's wisest monarch.— The PREACHER-KING seems to have exhausted the subtleties of human nature and reduced them to axioms in *Ecclesiastes.* When he declared that everything was vanity and vexation of spirit; that there had been, was, and would be nothing new under the sun; that the greatest services must expect nothing but ingratitude from individuals or communities; he was merely reducing to

4

philosophical sententiousness what Job, 1227 years before, had experienced, and what 2860 years have demonstrated as unalterable. Human means change, just as the *row-galley* has been succeeded by the *steamboat*, and the *mangonel*, by the *cannon ;*—human objects never :—

> "Men change with fortune, Manners change with climes,"
> "Tenets with books and Principles with times. :"—

nevertheless men's ends are always the same. The progress of human events advances, rolling on in circles, which may have been typified by the wheels—

> ———"Wheel within wheel undrawn,
> Itself instinct with spirit"

which Ezekiel saw in his magnificent vision upon the plains of *Chebar*. In accordance with this immutable law of progression, those who have read closely and reflected deeply will see that the events that have occurred in this, our, country are nothing new, but have had their parallels in the Free Governments of Ancient Times, in the Republics of the Middle Ages, in the federal career of the United Provinces of Holland, and, very especially, in the history of the Swiss Confederation. In the case of the last, the similitude is so wonderful that all whose attention has been called to the subject; have remarked and noted, almost in the same words, many successive, astonishing points of resemblance. Before entering however upon the particular parallel in history, one pertinent consideration should never be forgotten. Wherever a free government, invited or permitted foreign interference, that government was overthrown. The Monroe Doctrine is nothing more than a recognition of this immutable law, and, if energetically applied, it is an antidote to the poison of foreign intervention in the affairs of this, our continent ; ours by the law of nature, ours by the force of arms, as soon as victorious over treason we can give due attention to the intrusion of foreign enemies.

The minds of our youth have not been sufficiently directed to the study of history, *especially the history of foreign commonwealths*. The Rules and Axioms deducible from the Records of Nations, applied with common sense, can be relied with the same security as *Experience*. Republics however must learn from Republics. Any attempts to draw parallels between Republics and Monarchies will lead to fallacious results.

At the present time there is, besides the United States, but one real republic in the world. Nominal republics have arisen in abundance in the course of man's history, but the Federation of the Swiss cantons is the only one worthy to be named alongside of the great American experiment. The Spanish-American commonwealths are little better than anarchies. Of the three *quasi* European republics that existed before the French Revolution, all were extinguished by the arms of the first Napoleon.— Switzerland, however, still remains to bear witness on the Continent to the principles of self-government and the inextinguishable spirit of liberty.

The failure of former republics or commonwealths, and the occasional license or sporadic excesses of liberal institutions, should neither discourage nor disgust thinking men.

"LIBERTY," says MACAULAY "resembles the Fairy of Ariosto who, by some mysterious law of her nature, was condemned to appear at certain seasons in the form of a foul and poisonous snake. Those who injured her during the period of her disguise, were forever excluded from participation in the blessings which she bestowed. But to those who, in spite of her loathsome aspect, pitied and protected her, she afterwards revealed herself in the beautiful and celestial form which was natural to her, accompanied their steps, granted all their wishes, filled their houses with wealth, made them happy in love, and victorious in war. Such a Spirit is LIBERTY. At times she takes the form of a hateful reptile. She grovels, she hisses, she stings. But woe to those who in disgust shall venture to crush her! And happy are those who, having dared to receive her in her degraded and frightful shape, shall at length be rewarded by her in the time of her beauty and her glory."

"There is only one cure for the evils which new acquired freedom produces—and that cure is freedom!"

Again, hear to him!—

"Many politicians of our time are in the habit of laying it down as a self evident proposition, that no people ought to be free till they are fit to use their freedom. The maxim is worthy of the fool in the old story, who resolved not to go into the water till he had learned to swim! *If Men are to wait for Liberty till they become wise and good in Slavery, they may indeed wait forever.*"

Of the three European Republics, *Holland*, *Venice* and *Genoa*, destroyed by the great NAPOLEON, that modern Attila, the fate of the first, *Holland*, is most sad to contemplate.

It would be wise for the people of these United States to reflect upon the results of partisan spirit and intestine conflicts in a country, which, while it occupied an almost imperceptible space upon an ordinary map of the world, but *while it was yet* TRUE *to itself*, exercised the influence of a power of the first class, and like the diminutive-bodied but powerful *polypus*, embraced and held fast the richest and remotest regions in the tenacious grasp of its Briarian arms.

Hollands armor of proof was torn open by the violence of her own political factions to receive the foreign thrust which deprived her of existence as a republic.

It is painful even to read what exactions Holland suffered, at the hands of those who styled themselves her Emancipators. The result was, that a Commonwealth, which had planted its victorious banners, amid the roar of artillery, within the Arctic circle, when it fought the English off Spitzbergen; which had blanched the cheeks of London with the broadsides of its triumphant navy, master of the Thames; which had founded a NEW *Amsterdam* on this continent, a POLAR *Amsterdam* in *East Greenland*, now *Spitzbergen*, and a JAVANESE *Amsterdam* in the spice producing East; which had kept the "*Feast of Kings*" in *Nova Zembla*; which had dotted the globe with its discoveries and acquisitions; which had heaped a whole town *La Cidade* or *Pavoassan*, as a monument, upon the grave of a beloved admiral, under the equator; which had governed a modern empire, Brazil, as a dependent colony; which had chastised the Barbary Corsairs while still a terror to the mightiest monarchies; which had held at bay the armies, and vanquished the united fleets of France and Britain; fell from her place of pride and from a mighty republic, the arbitress of Europe, sunk into a third rate monarchy. From her misfortune, DAVIES, the elegant historian of the Dutch nation, deduces the following lesson—a lesson which should be thundered in the ears of our people in the public squares, and impressed upon their minds in the private circle—a lesson pregnant with significance to every American at this terrible epoch.

"From her place of pride, among nations, *Holland* has now fallen; and in the history of her fall, may be read a useful, though melancholy lesson to every free and com mercial people, to be on the watch lest *they mistake the heat of party spirit, for the zeal of patriotism: and lest they seek for national wealth as the* END, *and not as the* MEANS, *of national greatness."*

Holland's catastrophe is but one additional proof that the disease, fatal to republics, never had its origin in extraneous causes, although the mortal blow may have been eventually given from without.

Some free states have perished like fruit, prematurely ripe, or ripe out of season, just as HUSS, SAVANAROLA, and other Reformers suffered at the stake, because they were in *advance* of the age in which they lived, while ZWINGLI, LUTHER and CALVIN survived to see their doctrines flourish having taken the times at the turn of the tide, or at the flood. From the failure of foreign and former republics, men have argued, that freedom in government is incompatible with human existence, in great aggregations and developments, even as a congeries or family of confederated republics. Switzerland has solved the problem on a small scale. The United States is now solving a similar problem on a grand scale. Woe to mankind, if we, the latter, fail to do our Duty.

The Swiss Republic, in one respect, that is in their determined rejection of foreign interference in their domestic affairs, presented a perfect contrast to the Dutch. The result is, Switzerland exists in honored independence. Holland on the other hand, submitted to foreign intervention, and shorn of her liberty, subsists in comparative subservience.

The Swiss absolutely refused, at any risk and at all times, to permit the slightest interference on the part of foreign governments, and when in 1847 they had established their blockade or *cordon*, they actually prohibited to foreign agents, all access to their rebel districts. And while they were ready to mass their troops, to put down sedition at home, they were equally ready to mass their troops upon their frontiers, to prevent intervention from abroad. As an evidence to what exertions this patriotic spirit incited the people consider the case of the canton of *Vaud.* This canton has a population of 204,000 in an area of 1185 square miles. Taking the usual ratio her regular contingent, permanently maintained, should not exceed 5,000 men, and her males capable of bearing arms, between 20 and 60, not over 50,000 men, for home service and under the most favorable circumstances. Nevertheless, Oct. 2d, 1846, the same year that the SONDERBUND promulgated their treasonable designs, this canton had nearly 20,000 men, belonging to the different services, armed and equipped according to regulation. Besides these, the authorities had organized 16 Battalions of "Hommes du Depot," garrison troops between 17 and 20 years of age, (each 500 strong,) and 8 battalions of Volunteers, between the ages of 45 and 60, estimated as high as 6,000 in all: Total 34,000. The same proportion would give us 3,000,-000 of soldiers under arms, while the ability to bear the burthen can scarcely be brought into comparison.

This proves that in whatever other respect the Swiss may have retrograded, they have not degenerated in patriotism. Mrs. STRUTT, in her charming volumes, entitled "A Domestic Residence in Switzerland," observes that "Nature certainly only meant the Swiss for two classes, soldiers and shepherds." "Attached *alike to Liberty and to Arms,* the slightest appearance of infringement upon their freedom, throws them simultaneously into a posture of defence."

"The great tie that holds the Swiss cantons together is the neutrality they observe, with respect to other nations :

and the *common cause they make of* ANY *attack upon themselves.*"

"'Another admirable trait of *essential union* among the Swiss, is the willing and ready CHARITY with which they minister to each others wants, in times of calamity,' 'with a liberality that well illustrates the truth of a remark, which all who have studied mankind must have made, that it is always the habitually frugal, who are capable of the most generous actions."

> " Seek not the Swiss in cultured plains,
>   Or towns, or beaten paths among,
>   Where modish strangers idly throng.
> And luxury taints, and avarice stains:
> 'Tis where primeval nature reigns,
>   Mid lonely toil and simple song,
>   Secure alike from crime and wrong,
> He uncorrupt and true remains ;
>   'Mid the murmurings of his fountains.
>   And the echoes of his mountains,
> Where the lordly eagle soars,
> Where the headlong torrent roars,
>   He is, as he was meant to be,
>   Poor and virtuous, calm and FREE."

The prodigious effort of the little Canton of *Vaud* just alluded to, leads to the consideration of what would seem to be a want of sense of patriotic duty, in many of our own people.

Through the ill judged interference of rich communities or associations, the administration is not deriving the expected reinforcements from the draft just concluded.— That so many citizens are unwilling to fight out, with their own arms, the great battle of freedom, but are willing to confide it to another race, and hireling hands, is unworthy of a free people, and teeming with mischief, if no remedy is at hand and applicable.

I particularly allude to the organization of a disproportionate army of blacks. Their undue augmentation is pregnant with evil, if not restricted within reasonable limits. Not that I am opposed to negro regiments. Far from it, since I believe that I was the first, in print, to suggest their organization. But I am opposed to a negro army outnumbering that composed of whites. *Carthage, Venice, Holland,* relied upon mercenaries to maintain their polity within, extend their area without, and fight even for their independence. Rome's *mobilized militia* burned *Carthage;* the *native* armies of France seized *Venice,* and handed her over to *Austria* as a prey; and *Holland,* dictated to by *Prussia* and *England,* (the latter as false to the *United Provinces,* as she has proved to the *United States,*) stooped her free neck to the yoke of royalty; stooped it to be abased a second time, and plundered in 1830-'1, *despite their own solemn quarantees,* by *England* and *France,* just as *England* and *France* would like to dismember, plunder and humiliate us. The rough edge of the work may be taken off by our black auxiliaries, but the finishing touches must be put on by ourselves, by our white brethren.

Thus by the consideration of a succession of introductory suggestions, having an important bearing on the subject, I have reached in order the main object of my Address.

It is remarkable that Switzerland, a few years ago, was called upon to pass through a crisis very similar to that through which the United States is now passing. As a Federation it is composed of Cantons of quite dissimilar religious faith and social tendencies. Some of them are Protestants and others are Romanists, and the political jealousies which arise are apt to be intensified, if we may use the expression, by the antagonism of a deep religious rancor. On most questions, however, the Federal Diet would move along evenly enough if these causes of difference were not worked upon and fomented by dextrous, unrelenting and bigoted bodies of men, particularly by that known as the Jesuits. In political cunning, recklessness and energy, they are not unlike the southern disunion leaders ; and they are like them, again, in the fact' that for many years they were constant plotters of Secession.— They were always striving to arouse the prejudices of the Romanist cantons, until they should formally declare their separation from the others and from the general union.

Nor were foreign influences wanting to aggravate the internal difficulties. The Pope afforded aid by intrigues, carried on through his Nuncios, who incited the ignorant mass. The secession party comprised the whole of that part of the population which, dwelling in wild and mountain districts, had not been affected by the improvements of the age. They resembled in these respects the great mass of the southern secessionists, who live apart from the civilizing influences of commerce and intellectual pursuits. Austria helped also, not by mere hints, but open threats of intervention. She supplied arms, ammunition, and even officers. The staff of the secessionists was chiefly composed of foreign officers. France, likewise, smuggled arms and ordnance stores into the disaffected districts.— All the governments with despotic tendencies, in fact, either openly or secretly supported the secessionists.— Even constitutional governments, with the exception of England, gave the national party the cold shoulder. Thus abetted, a Sonderbund, as it was called, assembled for deliberation in May, 1846, and promulgated their Secessionist Confederacy.

MEMBERS OF THE VERMONT HISTORICAL SOCIETY and CITIZENS of the famed GREEN MOUNTAIN STATE, DESCENDANTS of the GREEN MOUNTAIN BOYS who distinguished themselves by their stern determination and intrepid enterprise in the times which tried men's souls, I shall endeavor, upon this occasion, to show you how another people, Sons of the Mountains, met the question of *Secession*. They met it as I have no doubt you would have met it, as all RURAL *New England* and RURAL *New York* would have met it, had they stood alone, fair and square, face to face, even as previous generations in the same districts asserted their rights on the fields of BENNINGTON and ORISKANY, STILLWATER (Bemus' Heights) and SARATOGA (Wilbur's Basin).

Before entering into any examination of historical occurrences, or of military operations which have taken place in Switzerland, a few remarks are pertinent to correct a popular error in regard to the defensibleness, *per se*, of that country, and, in fact, of any country presenting a similar physical aspect such as *Western Virginia, Tennessee* and *Georgia*. The plains of Italy and the levels of the Low Countries have been scarcely more fought over than the diversities and alternations of Switzerland. ZSCHOKKE, a German by birth but a Swiss by election, in his history of his adopted country, remarks that in its wars of the last 500 years, but particularly those growing out of the *great French Revolution*, "battle field touched battle field;" that "horse and man (contending) passed over the mountain tops, which the chamois hunter alone had reached before;" that "in the valleys and on the summits of the mountains, on the lakes and above the clouds, the French and Austrians fought."

Surrounded by powerful, ambitious, and military monarchies, Switzerland for centuries has been the "Valley of Decision," and the iron-heel of war has left its mark upon her snowy wastes, her vine clad slopes, her sunny valleys, and her romantic lake and river shores. From the summit of every Alp, deemed accessible, seventy years since, to man, to the bottom of her defiles, there is scarcely a district that has not been drenched with the blood of native and of foreign soldiery, recruited from almost every known region of Europe, Asia and northern Africa.

According to the hypothetical strategy of the newspapers and of the masses, positions in mountain ranges and mountainous countries, militarily occupied, are considered impregnable. Whereas it is a military axiom, established by the experience of all ages, that he who is master of the valleys is master of the mountains, for, although the mountains may not be susceptible of successful *direct* attack, they may be paralyzed by the cutting off of communications and conquered by blockade and famine.— This is indisputable except, in some rare cases, where mountain districts contain, or produce, within themselves supplies of ammunition, food and forage.*

Perhaps the most remarkable instance of this is Frederic the Great's operations against the impregnable Camp of Refuge at Pirna, in Saxony, in 1756. Master of the communications and victorious over the Austrian army,

* This remarkable fact, so seldom considered,—that the possession or mastership of the valleys determines the fate of mountains,—indicates the Rents or Gashes in the apparently invulnerable armor of an Alpine land. Through the Gaps by which the torrent finds escape, the enemy finds entrance. They offer to the invader breaches through which his columns can advance against the Penetralia of Liberty. Even as the treacherous arrow of the Trojan Adulterer, Paris, found its way, through the undipped heel, to the life of the otherwise invulnerable Achilles, even so the enemy finds access, by its Passes or Cols (depressions of the mountain crest lines into the interior of an elevated country), not only in arms but with the more fatal lures of trade and the blandishments of luxury.

The very Configuration of Switzerland and the disposition of its natural ramparts indicate, upon the map, the breaches through which its enemies have forced their way. It is least defensible towards the North and North-East. From those quarters the majority of the invasions have occurred. Happily for the Confederation its lofty barren mountains inclose luxuriant vineyards, meads and fields, furnishing vast supplies for men and cattle. On the other hand the Protestants of Languedoc, who held at bay for years the vast power of Louis XIV, occupied a territory resembling Switzerland in its capabilities for defence, but not analogous in its interior features of productiveness. The War of the Cevennes demonstrated what a determined Few, although unprepared, can achieve, for a time, against the Many provided with all sufficient means. There is a period, however, to all such efforts which is beyond the control of any will, however resolute. As long as they had seeking to relieve the Saxon forces, he compelled the latter to surrender at discretion, in about 37 days. Nevertheless Pirna, *per se*, was impregnable. We will see that the same rule has always held good with regard to Switz-ERLAND, and that, throughout the history of the Confederation, its fate has not been decided on its rugged Alps or in its mountain Thermopylæ's, but in its gladsome valleys, those depressions which give access to the interior of the country, and are traversed by the main-routes between the capitals or chief towns of the Cantons.

Strange it is, but still as true as strange, the ARTS OF WAR and the ARTS OF PEACE are subject to the same immutable laws of progress. WATER, WEALTH and WAR seek the same channels for their fertilizing streams or devastating floods. They equally shun the rugged heights and seek the fertile plains, for they are mutually dependent. Battle fields, invariably occur in localities which have the same relations to the Operations of War which towns or the sites of great fairs bear to the tides of Travel and Commerce. The result is that as Holland opposed dykes of granite, oak and concrete to the inroads of the

the means to support life, the Camisards of JOHN CAVALIER continued masters of their mountain fastnesses, and proved victorious against astonishing odds of men and material. When at length want obliged them to descend into the plains in search of supplies, they were overwhelmed by the disciplined masses of their royalist persecutors. Decimated through the efforts and effects of their own valor, they were at length compelled to retreat. Close upon them followed death and desolation, for the King's forces laid everything in ruins and ashes as they advanced. Thus a desert closed in upon the Huguenot heroes like the iron walls of the Italian tyrants daily diminishing dungeon, until, at last, all within the encompassing and converging columns of the invader was crushed into submissive formlessness in respect to rights or religion and to individual or general security. SCHAMYL, in like manner, as the Protestants of the Cevennes, found his Circassian strongholds assailed by Russian armed floods surging up through the Circassian valleys which opened to the lowlands and to the sea, commanded by the Czaric fleets.

Just so, the Deluges of Asiatic barbarism which overwhelmed Eastern and Central Europe followed the levels of the rivers, and burst in upon Christianity and Civilization through the depressions of the border ranges, through which Commerce had found lines of communication, proving that the Traffic and Strife, both bearing with them good and evil, in very unequal proportions however, tread the same tracks either to bless or blast.

ocean, so Switzerland dammed her valleys against the invasions of multitudinous enemies with ranks of *iron* men,
so that it might be said of HELVETIA as of the SPARTA of
AGESILAUS and the SWEDEN of the VASAS, "She did not
defend her men with walls, but her walls with her men."

Although the swarthy crisp-haired veterans of HANNI-
BAL picked and fought their way through the icy terrors
of Mount Genevre (or the Little St. Bernard?);—

Although the Emperor MAJORIAN, sounding the depths
of the drifts with the staff of his lance, indicated, in mid-
winter, the track for the march of his legions, fresh from
battling with the savage Moors and Vandals, across the
Graian Alps, to the conquest of Gaul, Spain and
Africa;—

Although FRANCIS I. tunneled the Monte Viso, far
under its perpetual snow, deeming the very rocks less
impervious than the ranks of their WALDENSIAN defenders,
on his way to that " Combat of Giants," Marignano ;—

Although the veteran FREUNDSBERG threaded the horrible snow depths and yawning ravines of the Val Sabbia,
at the head of that " Army of Vengeance " which repaid
itself, with the accumulated gold of papal jubilees, for
the spiritual tyranny and humiliations which Germany
had experienced at the hands of the Popes ;—

Although PRINCE EUGENE transported " in a fearful
and marvellous march," with the help of mechanical
contrivances, his infantry, cavalry, and even artillery,
through the frightful Val Suga and Val Fredda, hitherto
deemed inaccessible, to rescue his patrial Savoy from the
closing grasp of the French spoiler ;—

Although the Muscovites, under the barbarian SUWAR-
ROW, trampled the eternal snow of the St. Gothard and
replaced the Devil's Bridge with trunks of trees lashed
together with his officers' military sashes ;—

Although the Gallic demi-brigades of NAPOLEON trod into slush the everlasting snow of the Great St. Bernard, hurrying forward to his greatest victory, Marengo ;—

Although the exhilarating music of MACDONALD's military bands excited his French divisions to charge the falling avalanches of the Splugen as if they had been columns of mortal adversaries ;—

Although I say from the days of the *Carthaginian Arch-strategist* to those of the Conqueror of *Solferino*, horse, foot, elephants, cannon and military equipages have fought their way, across the Alps, to victory, by the tracks of the hunter and the paths of the goat-herd ;—

Although cavalry and artillery have charged upon fields of ice, *above the clouds*, and answered, amid the mingled wreaths of vapor and powder-smoke, the electric batteries of nature with their batteries of human invention ;—yet

The fate of Switzerland has not been decided in her elevated mountain passes and upon her hoary Alps, but in her smiling valleys and along the shores of those lakes, which were alive with a semi-aquatic population, living in huts elevated on piles above their waters, anterior to the age of bronze and iron, and while her mountains were yet devoid of inhabitants.

In *one* respect, however, mountainous countries are impregnable. Territories, like those of the Swiss, are inexpugnable in the race of men which grow up amid the sublimity of their scenery. "Solitude," says the philosophic prose-poet, Dora d'Istria, "is the mother of great ideas." We add, Sublimity is certainly their father in minds susceptible of quickening.

The mountain race, endowed with vigorous minds in healthy bodies, seems everywhere gifted with an indomitable resolution, as rugged and flinty as the rocks they have to climb and labor among in the pursuit of their livelihood.

Moreover, just as we recognize an elevated region by its sturdy growth of peculiar timber, whether stunted or lofty, alike in their power of resisting the tempest, and by its hardy plants, characterized by their intense tenacity of life, just so a mountainous country is indicated by a sturdy, courageous, athletic, well developed or close knit population of liberty-loving, patriotic men.

During the American Revolution it was the mountaineers of Eastern Tennessee, South-Eastern Kentucky, and Western North, and South, Carolina, who stemmed the tide of British conquest in the Southern provinces, although led by its ablest and boldest partisan, bull-dog FERGUSON. When the South Carolinian oligarchic chivalry and its aristocracy, rich in human chattels, had entirely succumbed, it was the energy, sagacity and self reliance of the *Mountain Men*, accustomed to manual labor and exercised in their contests with savage beasts and still more savage men, which restored affairs and even hope, by their unexpected success, upon the bloodiest scene of Southern battle, the ever memorable *Kings Mountain*.

Just so, in this very State, Gentlemen, *New Hampshire* and *Vermont* troops, under the simple but intrepid Stark, ratified at *Bennington*, the great fundamental principle of government, that neither the Green Mountain region, nor any other region, should be the home of any but free-men. The same spirit inspired the rough but patriotic ALLEN, when he laid his iron grasp upon Ticonderoga "in the name of the great Jehovah and the Continental Congress." The same spirit, with its impulse as potential as the shrill note of the Abyssinian trumpet, styled the *Cry of the*

Eagle, whose electric effect is dwelt upon by the traveller BRUCE, as marvellous to witness, aroused Vermont to arms at the commencement of the pending contest.

The Voice of the same Spirit, resounding through the Green Mountains, as irresistibly as the appeal of the *Mountain Horn* or *Bull of Uri,* whose terrible roar resembled the bellowing of the enraged *Urus,* and of the hoarse *Land Horn* of *Unterwalden,*—whose signals struck terror to the enemies of Switzerland who had experienced their effects,—summoned together, and urged forth, under such leaders as JOHN WOLCOTT PHELPS, a magnificent array, exceeding in numbers the proportionate quota of your State, small in area and population, however great in virtues, a contingent, far more excessive in the quality of its soldiers, to fight the great fight of freedom, upon the soil, which the treason of a slavocrat-oligarchy sought to usurp and subject to the fatal influences of slavery,— hoping to build, there, upon the ruins of our free institutions, an aristocracy based upon their ownership in man.

Even as your lovely state is intersected by fertile valleys, watered by such beautiful streams as the WINOOSKI, MISSISQUI, and WHITE River, whose banks afford easy transit to the iron horse dragging long trains, freighted with the spoils of commerce and of agriculture, even so Switzerland is cleft and checkered by connecting depressions, the basins of its chains of lakes, gleaming like diamonds or sapphires amid the cloud-crowned mountains, snow-capped peaks, elevations robed in ever verdant foliage, and glaciers spectral in their ice, when not glorious, like Iris, in the sunshine.

It is these very velvet pastures and rich meadows, bathed by the Swiss lakes and their tributaries, so dear to the tourist, the agriculturist and the herdsman, which have afforded fields of manœuvre and battle to the chivalry of the invaders, seeking to enslave their possessors. Upon such slopes and meadows, most of the Swiss battles of their wars of independence have been decided. Such depressions, alone, have offered stages for the vast conflicts, which have occurred from time to time, during the last 600 years, whence the thundering antagonism of the artillery, reverberating through the encompassing mountains, have jarred loose the dreadful avalanches to respond with the still more terrible echo of their fall, to the roar of the contending hosts below.

    *   *   *   *   *   *   *

In the progress of our consideration of this subject—*Swiss Secession*—it appears to me that this would be the proper time, before proceeding farther, or entering upon the narrative of actual hostilities, to trace out the origin of the difficulty by a brief examination of the History of the *Helvetian Republic.*

The *Swiss Confederation*, born, 1291, in the *Association of the Three Forest Cantons*, on the *Lake of Lucerne*, grew, in 1352, to *Eight* by gradual aggregations. Baptised in blood and fire, to use a military expression, it already constituted, in the XIVth Century, a strong family of small republics.

These had gained over Austria a series of victories, whose parallels cannot be found in history. Still, although it had vanquished the empire, its arch enemy without, it could not overcome enemies almost as dangerous, although not so apparent, within ; the blemishes, cruelties and vices of its interior administration. The tyranny of oligarchs had been permitted to succeed that of feudalism. Spiritual foundations still held the fortunes, rights, and what was far worse, the minds of their subjects in the fetters of superstition and ignorance. The terrible yoke of caste hung heavily upon the population, and nothing but the discipline, as it were, of a frontier post, exposed to the danger of attack at any moment, kept the different populations of *Freedom's Citadel*, in Central Europe, from flying at each other's throats upon the least occasion. The exciting cause of disunion has ever been the same as that which lately stirred up SWISS SECESSION,—the intrigues of the Church of Rome, of its allies, of its affiliations and of its dependencies, in a word the ULTRAMONTANE or REACTIONIST PARTY, not inaptly represented, in this country, by the SLAVOCRATS and their abettors.

In 1444, France succeeded Austria as the antagonist of Freedom and of the Cantons, and met with such a bloody reception at St. Jacob on the Birs, on the very threshold of the confederation, that, thenceforward, until her own great Revolution, the French rulers were willing rather to *buy* the amity than to *provoke* the enmity of the Swiss.

Unwilling or incapable of profiting by the experience of the astute LOUIS XI, his opponent, CHARLES *the* RASH of BURGUNDY, determined to try *his* hand at oppressing Switzerland. Burgundy, although a feudal duchy, was, yet, at that time, a kingdom in power and influence, although its sovereign wore only a ducal coronet. Moreover, the army with its train of artillery and equipages, which, twice renewed and twice entirely ruined, CHARLES poured over the Jura into what was then the Canton of BERNE, would be termed magnificent even at the present day. Two defeats, so marvellous and overwhelming, that nothing but the more recent routs of ROSBACH, LEUTHEN, JENA, the annihilation of the whole French expedition to Moscow, WATERLOO and NOVARA, could justify belief in the disasters which shipwrecked the fame, the power and the armies of *Burgundy*. A third victory, NANCY, in 1477, cost the magnificent CHARLES his life.

At this period of triumph, in 1481, SOLEURE and FREY-BURG, contrasts in their after political conduct, were admitted into the Confederation as the ninth and tenth Cantons.

Despots and kings, and, in fact, political administrations of every texture, never appear to learn wisdom from the past. To impose the Austrian yoke, upon the TEN Cantons, which his ancestors could not impose upon THREE, or upon FOUR, or upon EIGHT, the German Emperor took the field in person.

Defeated by the Swiss in not less than eight battles in the course of as many months, MAXIMILIAN resolved upon peace. He had lost over twenty thousand men and seen nearly two thousand towns, villages and castles laid in ashes to satisfy his ambitious attempts upon liberty.— Peace accordingly was concluded at BASLE, September 22d, 1499. Thus ended the *Suabian*, the last war of Swiss independence. These wars had dragged out through two hundred and one years. The American Wars of Independence, if we consider, as many do, the War of the Revolution as the First or Inceptive, and the War of 1812 as the Second or Decisive, forty-five years. The first blood shed in the American Revolution, was not in King's Street, Boston, March 5th, 1770, nor at Lexington, *April* 19th 1775, but on GOLDEN HILL, in John Street, in New York City, January 18th 1770, preceding by two months, the first New England martyr-dom for liberty. The last conflict to establish our *complete* independence of Great Britain was at NEW ORLEANS, January 8th, 1815.

The first struggle of the Swiss Revolution was on the DONNERBUHL (Thunder Hill) and in the *Jammerthal* (Vale of Tears), appropriate names, in 1298; the last victory at DORNACH in 1499. It must be conceded the Swiss had a harder fight, against greater odds, for their Freedom, than we, Americans, for ours. What is acquired with great difficulty is highly esteemed. The Swiss have maintained their freedom and consolidated their unity. Will we emulate their example? -

From that Treaty of BASLE dates, properly speaking, the complete independence of Switzerland, which then ceased to be subjected to the sovereignty of the empire—a state of things which was sanctioned by the PEACE OF WEST-PHALIA, in 1648.

The French War, of 1444, had been a mere August thunder shower, fierce enough, however, while it lasted; the Burgundian War, of 1475-'6-'7, a succession of tornadoes; the Suabian War, 1499, was a regular, furious storm, but the Cantons sustained the violence of all three as the Alps meet the *Fœhn* and the *Bise*, two furious winds peculiar to Switzerland, whose blasts accomplish nothing but to purify the air.

In 1501, BASLE and SCHAFFHAUSEN were admitted as the eleventh and twelfth, and in 1515, APPENZELL as the last Canton necessary to complete the list of the *first Thirteen*, exactly the number of the British Provinces which transmuted themselves into the original THIRTEEN United States.

Of these *Thirteen* three were *Aristo-Democratic*. The first of these was ZURICH, afterwards the home of liberal ideas and the cradle of the Reformation. In consideration of the wealth and importance of the City of Zurich, the others yielded to it the first place in order of rank,

and it has ever since borne the title, although it long since
lost the prerogative, of the first Canton of the Helvetic
body. This privilege, however, gave Zurich no superiority over the rest, but merely constituted it as a central
point, where all the affairs, which concerned the whole
confederation, were transacted ; its deputies had also for
a time the precedency in the general diets.

Of the other two, the most important, BASLE, was then
what it proved in the last Swiss Secession War, neither
cold nor hot, as we shall see hereafter, looking only, like
all commercial emporiums, to its own selfish interests.

Of the four Aristocratic Cantons, BERNE was subsequently, 1798—1803, divided into four, and afterwards
became one of the most Liberal or *Democratic*, perhaps,
for the same reason, that SAMSON became weak. *Her*
extensive dependencies, like *his* long locks, the sources of
her strength, having been shorn off by the very reactionary
power, whose influences adverse to Liberty, had laid her
to sleep.

Two others, LUCERNE and FREYBURG, have always been
the enemies of progress, and completely in the hands of
those whose interests it was to keep the people bigoted
and ignorant. In 1782, Freyburg was the *closest aristocracy* or rather *oligarchy* in all Switzerland, and one of the
most bigoted. Latterly, it scarcely ceded to *Lucerne* in
that regard.

The fourth, SOLEURE, situated in the valley of the *Aar*,
has been liberalized in a measure by the commerce and
travel, foreign especially, flowing through it.

The six *Democratic* Cantons hardly exceeded in area
or population either of the *Aristocratic ;* in wealth there
was no comparison. Jealous of their own liberties, they
had little respect for the liberties of others where those

liberties conflicted with their own political prejudices and religious bigotry. This always led them to become members of each successive Secession League—(for every secession League was formed to arrest Liberality in Sentiment and Politics,)—and become the Associates of Coalitions with Despotic tendencies. It is singular that the rule which governs unions between parties, the most dissimilar in their habits and feelings, but identical in apparent interests, holds good not only in private life, in marriages, but in public life, in national alliances. Witness our own predilections for the Russian government, the most despotic in Europe, while yet we were on the closest terms of amity with *England*, and in numerous other instances. Even autocratic Romanist France was preferred to constitutional Protestant Great Britain.

Besides these, there were subject *Bailiwicks*, and *Confederate States*, known as *Socii, Associates* or *Allies*, subsequently, from time to time, embraced within the limits of the present twenty two Cantons. Three *Aristo-Democratic*, four *Aristocratic* and six *Democratic* Cantons constituted this Alliance, rather than actual Confederation of Thirteen States, which bound together by a general alliance, were still not, in all cases, allied to each other. Incongruous as it was in many respects, it lasted nevertheless, with modifications, but no essential changes down to the end of the XVIIIth Century. From 1516 to 1718, from the time when ZWINGLI commenced to preach the gospel, when as yet the name of LUTHER had never been heard of in Alpine districts,—that is from the inception of the Reformation in Switzerland, down to the religious Peace of AARAU,—was a period of continual intestine struggles, excited and instigated by the same religious jealousies, oppressions and antipathies; demons which have only been laid by the magic of the sword within six years.

From the PEACE OF AARAU, in 1712, (which is generally credited to 1718, since the Abbot of St. Gall did not accede to it until six years after its agreement,) down to 1798, the Cantons enjoyed the blessings of seventy nine years of comparative repose. In the winter of 1797–'8, the French troops invaded the Cantons. This year, 1798, Lavater styled the first year of Swiss Slavery, which may be said to have lasted fifteen to seventeen years. In 1798, the old confederate bond was loosed by the French. It had stood the strain of four hundred and ninety years; in seventy four days it was now dissolved.

The cantons which composed the first Association of the XIIIth Century contained the germs of future difficulties, similar to those which existed in a dormant state within our own confederation from its inception. These seeds of discord were sufficiently apparent in the country to occasion more prophecies of our present contest than those emitted by LORD COLERAINE and by BURKE, within a few years after the adoption of the Federal Constitution. In Switzerland the remnant of abuses, privileges oppressions, as old as the organization of its primitive government, had a great deal to do with Secession, but in both countries, which it has cursed, the object was the same—*the aggrandizement of a governing caste* of aristocratic and spiritual oligarchs at the expense of their fellow men. In Switzerland, as in America, a dominant class sought to impose their yoke not only upon matter but upon mind.

Although SECESSION, visibly, dates back only to CALHOUN, in 1832, when it bore the title of NULLIFICATION, it nevertheless existed, as a latent idea, in the shape of STATE RIGHTS in the minds of many of those who signed the first Act of our Confederation. Just so in Switzerland. The Reformation was Anti-Slavery in *intent ;* the dominant church then Pro-Slavery in *effect.* The result was a Sonderbund or Secession spirit, which like some chronic diseases, assumed more or less violent phases under mitigating or aggravating circumstances. The exciting cause in the Sonderbund cantons, the seat of the difficulty or the organ affected, was never radically cured, although the remedies applied were sufficiently active or effectual to restrain the disease within certain limits. Finally foreign influence, like malarious air, against which Zwingli boldly sounded the alarm, developed the latent sentiment into contagious virulence.

Meanwhile, neglect on the part of the *family physician* the Federal Diet, permitted the difficulty to gain such a head that the cure required a medicine, (artillery pills, and bayonet lancets,) so violent in itself, that had the applications failed to effect a prompt cure, the practice would have destroyed the life of the *patient,* the *Swiss Confederation.*

Still another brief recapitulation of some events appears necessary at this time to make this question or analogy more intelligible. Secession, in Switzerland, was no more a *new* idea in 1846-'47 than it was in the United States, in 1860-'61. In 1528, the Legislature of Berne issued an Edict of Religious Reformation, in Thirteen Articles, founded on a truly Evangelical basis. This spiritual reform had just the same effect then, as the politico-spiritual ameliorations of the present century, particularly those called for between 1840 and 1847.— The Bernese regulations, conceived in a spirit of justice, charity and liberality, gave rise, in the November of the same year, to the League of the Valais, or Sonderbund of the five Romanist Cantons and the confederate State of the Valais for the defence of the

Romanist faith. FREYBURG joined the league afterwards.
In this SEPARATE LEAGUE we have the identical *Sonderbund* of 1847, excited by the very same causes, and
influenced by the same objects. What renders the resemblance more striking is, that just as the hereditary
enemy of Switzerland, FERDINAND of *Austria*, was admitted as a member of the Alliance of 1528, just so
Austria was the power and Austrian princes the agents
on which the treasonable alliance of 1846-'7 especially
relied for material support. "This alliance startled the
other Cantons. Alarm filled men's minds. They sung
the personal complaint everywhere:—

> " Wail Helvetians, Wail,
> For the Peacock's plume of Pride
> To the Forest Canton's savage Bull
> In Friendship is allied."

To parry the effects of this Separate League, ZURICH and
BERNE and other Reformed districts entered into what
they called a CHRISTIAN CO-BURGHERSHIP, in 1529, to which
Schaffhausen and *Basle* virtually acceded, in the following year, 1530. Three Cantons, divided within themselves,
remained more or less neutral. In the array of parties,
and in the condition of affairs in the XVIth Century, we
have a perfect type of what occurred in the XIXth. The
same antagonism has occurred with a greater or less resemblance more than once since between those eras, but
in 1530, Switzerland presented a perfect picture of the
Status of Romanism and Retrograde Tendencies, of Protes-
tantism and Liberal Progression, and of selfish Neutrality,
in exactly the same proportions, as occurred three hundred
and seventeen years later.

The first great French revolution which did so much
harm, accomplished, nevertheless, an immense deal of
good. The decree of the French Directory declaring that
the Swiss Confederation had ceased to exist, and organ-

izing Switzerland into a single republic with a central government, was not without its beneficial effects. The French revolution commenced that process of amalgamation, which the triumph over Secession in 1847 carried another step forward. It crushed Switzerland into something like a nationality which was a comparative blessing. It swept away castes and privileges, and substituted its own great despotism for the petty tyrannies previously existing. It failed because it lacked the true religious element, that is the religious element of the Bible, as many who watched its operations predicted, on account of that very omission, that it would fail.

"You may call a Republic of Unbelievers free, but that republican form confers no Liberty ; it may give scope to Licentiousness, but it can confer no Liberty. The land in which the mass rules is not a free land ; that is the Home of Freedom where Truth rules. That is no *true* Democracy in which all are on a level merely ; the *true* democracy is that in which all are Brothers—some elder, some younger, but all helping one another. *A democracy is impossible on any other than Christian principles.*"

Can any one deny that the masses in Europe are not better off to-day than they were before the French Revolution ? No sensible unprejudiced men would dare to do so. The outrages upon humanity then daily practiced by a dominant aristocracy and spiritual hierarchy are heard of no more. There are no more public or legalized tortures, there are no more dragonades, there are no more judicial murders like that of CALAS, at *Toulouse*, except in districts where the mind is still subjected to that yoke and frenzied by that goad, which brought about Swiss Secession, a spirit twin to that which occasioned our own Rebellion. We shudder at the wrongs inflicted upon our slaves. But if we are to believe VULLIEMIE and other authentic historians of Switzerland, the yoke of the negro was in the majority of cases lighter than that imposed by a dominant clergy and aristocracy upon their fellow whites. They speak of executions preceded by tortures which terrified the imagination, of mutilations and injustice worthy of the annals of Naples and of the Inquisition. A reader is tempted to throw down the book shocked at the recital of man's inhumanity to man. If any one questions these charges let him examine the Countess DORA D'ISTRIA's "Switzerland, the Pioneer of the Reformation," and her authorities.

All that was good in the French Revolution, its liberal elevating and regenerating influences can be traced to the operation of that Spirit which proclaimed release to the captive, quickened the Reformation, and declared that " where the Spirit of the Lord is there is Liberty,"— that Spirit whose purest modern exponent was ZWINGLI, the Swiss Reformer of ZURICH.

The horrors of the French Revolution were not its necessary or inevitable results. " Insensate resistance," DORA D'ISTRIA remarks in her German Switzerland, "compels Revolutionists to pass beyond the goal they would have been satisfied to reach. Were not the unceasing conspiracies of the clergy and of the aristocracy, and their dishonorable alliance with foreigners, the chief causes of the excesses of the French Revolution ?"

But to resume the regular narrative of events in Switzerland since 1795, which were interrupted by the preceding remarks.

In 1801, a Diet, assembled at Berne, proclaimed a Confederation of XVII Cantons with a *central* Federal government, in that city.

In 1803, BONAPARTE promulgated his Act of Mediation,

constituting Switzerland into a Confederation of XIX Cantons, with separate local governments and a Federal Diet for the whole.

In 1814, the Deputies of the majority of the Cantons, assembled at Zurich, proclaimed the Independence of the XIX Cantons as then existing. In this year the VALAIS, NEUFCHATEL, and GENEVA, were admitted as three new Cantons making the total, as at present, XXII.

In 1815 the Allied Powers, at the Congress of Vienna, acknowledged the Independence and Perpetual Neutrality of Switzerland, and a new Federal Compact of the XXII Cantons was sworn to in the Diet, at Zurich, in the August of that year.

The French Convention, and its successor the Directory, which transmuted the Seven United Provinces of Holland into the Batavian Republic (in 1795), the states of Northern and Central Italy into the Cisalpine Republic (in 1797,) and Southern Italy into the Parthenopeian Republic, (in 1798,) about the same time crushed together the Thirteen Swiss Cantons into the Helvetian Republic, (1797). Upon the final fall of Napoleon, Switzerland existed in a Bond of XXII Cantons, and, as such, it was recognized by the Congress of Vienna, which guaranteed its independence and perpetual Neutrality.

With the restoration of Switzerland's independence, recommenced the machinations of all those who were opposed to Liberal Institutions. Immediately again the disciples of Metternich and Talleyrand, sought to reunite the severed and tangled skein of intrigues, fomented by their predecessors, guiding spirits of the surrounding monarchical and despotic powers. Jealous of the existence of a successful Free State in their midst, Austria, France, and, in a much less degree, Prussia, had no sooner signed the guarantees of Swiss Independence, than they set to work to undermine it, and to divide the people, in the hope of annexing or appropriating any seceding or dissatisfied district, as they nearly succeeded in doing in 1846-'7.

It is greatly to be regretted that the limits of an Address precluded a more detailed examination of that Struggle, between Imperial and Papal Despotism, and comparative Freedom, which lasted from the first years of the XVI Century, to the Peace of Aarau (Argovia,) 1718; that struggle between spiritual darkness, and evangelical light which characterized the era of Zwingli, Luther and Calvin. That conflict between Lay and Ecclesiastical Aristocracy and Oligarchy and Democracy, which began with the beginnings of the Confederation, endured from the 15th Century, down to the Congress of Vienna, and was renewed, with almost equal bitterness, after Switzerland had recovered, at it were, her equilibrium, until, at length, enflamed by spiritual avidity for power, it blazed up into the Sonderbund troubles of 1840, and ended with the triumph of Republicanism, and the short, sharp, decisive, shattering triumph of the Liberals, Loyalists or Federalists, over Secession, in 1847.

Suffice it to say, that after the Recognition of the XXII Cantons, 20th March, 1815,—the renewed struggle of thirty years, between Swiss retrogradists, and progressionists, was characterized by a bitterness, which, in all likelihood, would have deterred many of our politicians from taking the stump, and embroiling public affairs.— They would have restricted their enthusiasm to *safer* occupations than statescraft, had they seen in the near future the Axe of the Headsman, and the Gyves of the Felon, as the almost certain rewards, in case of failure, of their interested endeavors. If the mountain begets fervor and fearless energy, it also begets ferocity and fierce zeal, even to the shedding of blood. Let us thank God, that hitherto we have been spared the sights of scaffolds, erected for those who have outraged the majesty of the constitution, instead of witnessing, as in Switzerland, the bloody block, and the grim headsman holding up the dripping head of the executed rebel.

The efforts at Nullification, in every regard, which began to show themselves in Switzerland, immediately upon the fall of Napoleon, were the origin of the Swiss Separate, or Secession League, (Sonderbund.) "The Separate League," said M. Druey, Deputy of Vaud, "is a continuation of the Reactionary Movement, of 1802 : of the Anti-national Intrigues of the Waldshut Committee (in 1812-'13); of the Aristocratic Enterprises of 1813-'14-'15; of the Conspiracy of 1832 ; of the Sarnen League in 1833 ; and of the Reaction effected in some Cantons since 1839, and attempted in others. That League would fain invade all the States of the Confederation."

Just as this REACTION in religious and political matters, permitted in certain Cantons, sought to invade and rule in more Liberal Cantons, just so *Slavery* endeavored to invade the Free States and impose and continue a succession of corrupt administrations upon our *free* North.

For thirty two years, Switzerland presented two hostile camps, which rested their extremities on foreign lands, and which attempted reciprocally to weaken each other, by the withdrawal of adherents. An attitude gradually more resolute and bolder was the result of these separate alliances.

According to the opinion of a writer, whose Christian sympathies and learning entitle her to reliance, the origin of the quarrel which brought these two camps into collision was the Suppression of the Convents of Argovia or

34

Aargau for taking part in political disturbances, in 1841,
on the motion of a Member of the Diet of their own
(Roman Catholic) persuasion.* Austria, which permits
no opportunity of exercising its reactionary influence in
the Swiss Confederation, interfered on the most frivolous
grounds. To avenge the Suppression of the Argovian
Convents, the Austro-Romanists or ULTRAMONTANISTS, by
which term we shall distinguish the REBELS or SECESSION
party in the Cantons, determined to invite the Jesuits to
return. The Ultramontanists held the balance of power
in Switzerland just, as it is to be feared, they do in this
country. To re-establish their influence this party recalled the Jesuits, whose Institution or Society, as early
as in 1818, had been energetically protested against, even
in bigoted Freyburg, as incompatible with a Free State.
The project of inviting this unpopular Society to Lucerne,
against the decided will of the majority of the Swiss people,
and the suggestion, at Lucerne, of the formation of a
SEPARATE LEAGUE or Sonderbund, for the armed maintenance of the peculiar views of the ULTRA-RETROGRADE
party, produced a formidable agitation throughout the
whole of Switzerland. This excitement engendered the
FREE CORPS, which bear the same relation to Swiss Secession that our armed Emigration to KANSAS bore to
the aggressions of Slavery. But just as the usurpations
and violences of Slavery produced such terrible results in
Kansas, just so the Ultra-party, in Switzerland, must be
held responsible for all that subsequently occurred there.
The discovery of the Minutes of the Separate-League
conspirators, of the 13th and 14th September, 1843, at
the Baths of ROTHEN, near LUCERNE, was a real triumph

* Compare MENZEL's *History of Germany* [in Mrs. Horrocks' Eng. Trans. (Bohn's
Edition), 1854], Chapter CCLXVIII, Pages 395-400 (particularly last ¶, Page 400),
Vol. III, with Countess DORA D'ISTRIA's *Switzerland, the Pioneer of the Reforma-
tion*, H. G.'s Trans., London, 1858, § XXIII, Pages 4-39, particularly 28-30, Vol. 2.

for the partisans of the Free Corps. It proved that the adversaries of the Volunteers, NOR *they*, had inaugurated the struggle. These Free Corps, however justifiable in principles and intention, were censurable in action.— Their invasion of Lucerne and the Valais was a parallel of JOHN BROWN's foray into Virginia without the lofty. enthusiasm and purity of purpose of the " hero of the Osawatomie." Moreover the expeditions of these Free Corps experienced the fate of John Brown's rash attempt. And just as his party were shot down at HARPER's FERRY in the name of SLAVERY, the Free Corps were shot down at the bridges across the TRIENT, the REUSS and the EMME, in the name of another, no less dangerous, slavery. These and similar successes over the Free Corps, particularly the bloody victory of the Ultramontanists at Lucerne, incited the conquerors to outrage all liberal sentiment and complete their preparations for the great struggle which they had determined to bring on, for, unless blind and stolid, they must have seen the terrible consequences which would ensue.

Let those who blame the operations of the Swiss Free Corps, or Volunteers, remember what bands of worse than savages, spiritual and political despots have often let loose upon Liberals ; let them recall the invasion of Kansas by hordes of Missourian desperadoes ; and let them recollect that no sooner had the Ultramontane coalition or Swiss *Sonderbund* gained the advantage over the Free Corps by the " Fratricide on the Trient," than *they actually forbade the practice of private worship, to Swiss Protestants, in* THEIR OWN *Canton.* "*The Grand Council of the Valais decided that the Roman Catholic religion alone* should a have worship *culte.*" LOUIS XIV had scarcely claimed more despotic authority over his Reformed subjects than the Ultramontanists exerted, where they had

the power of influencing citizens to tyrannize over their
fellow citizens. Zschokke says that now the assertion
of the Prebendary of Riraz was made good:—"That
Valais *first* of all was to be Catholic, *then* Swiss." As an
antithesis to this declaration bear in mind that the ex-
ponents of Slavery, at Richmond, assumed that any one
who did not believe in the divine institution of Chat-
telage, was an Abolitionist.

Thus it was made to appear to the world that the
Liberals inaugurated the contest, whereas the opposite
party had not only been long and secretly at work but
were actually prepared to receive the attacks upon Sion
and Lucerne which their crimes and conspiracies had occasioned. Are we not justified in stating that the summons to arms issued by the Rebel leaders invited and
justified a corresponding action in the Loyal party? The
Secessionists, both in Switzerland and the United States,
acted on the principle of Cardinal Richelieu, that "a Lie
which lasts four and twenty hours, makes great operation." This sentiment is attributed to Frederic the
Great, erroneously however. It did not originate with
the atheistical soldier, but with a Cardinal of that church
whose disciples dispersed to the winds the ashes of the
martyred Zwingli mingled with those of swine. The
Free Corps had the same plea for their organization and
action that European liberals, like Victor Hugo, admitted as valid in favor of John Brown. I am not here
to justify or condemn John Brown. I should not and I
would not presume even farther to discuss the subject.—
I have simply referred to it as an historical fact in order
to show how human events repeat themselves, even as to
details, and that, therefore, a critical study of history is
often equivalent to personal experience in a mind capable
of close analysis and comparison.

In many respects, even to particulars, the parallel between the ideas, assumptions and operations of the Swiss-Separate-League-Cantons and the American-Secession-States has been perfect. When Switzerland's War of Independence had been triumphantly terminated, ZWINGLI, the first and most practical of the Reformers, took his solemn stand against the Interventions of that Church, or rather Schism, which has been the Remittent Fever of the Confederation from his day to the present. In this prescience, he closely resembles our WASHINGTON, to whom Zwingli has been compared, in regard to his warnings against foreign influences and entangling alliances. Both alike were reverenced by the wise and the good everywhere, and respected and beloved at home.— Both were true patriots, devoted to the best interests of their several countries, and "magnanimous." What a vast scope of the highest eulogy does the last epithet, justly applied, embrace. Zwingli energetically protested, I repeat, with intrepid persistence against the lures and wiles of foreign incitations and entangling coalitions, and fell a victim to his foresight. His warnings were prophetic. The Influences, he denounced, as susceptible of producing such demoralizing consequences, equivalent to the effects of Slavery, were the causes of differences and bloodshed in Switzerland from his day to the present time, and even so Slavery, proper, has always kept our own country in a state of feverish excitement, and has ended in producing one of the bloodiest wars upon record. Alas, too soon for his country and the world, ZWINGLI fell a martyr to the animosity aroused by his patriotic eloquence.

Looking back two hundred and seventy years we find that the SONDERBUND of the XVIth Century known as the Borromean or GOLDEN LEAGUE of 1586, whose pretended object was simply mutual protection and assistance, was not only a defensive but likewise an aggressive alliance. Just so the SONDERBUND of 1843-'6. In our own case the Slave Party, its adherents and parasites, were never contented with the enjoyment of their own rights, but unceasingly endeavored to invade the prerogatives of others; to stem the tide of liberal progress and of freedom; and to acquire new guarantees for their very encroachments. In a lesser degree and sphere we have seen the same spirit germinate into the treasonable Association of the Knights of the GOLDEN CIRCLE, a fitting title, with an object analogous to that of the Golden League, the violation of the Constitution, the extension of slavery, and the subversion of Liberty.

Just as the Ultramontanists of Switzerland first violated the spirit and transgressed the limits of Federal compact, just so the Slavocrat political leaders eluded the restraints of the American Constitution. Their unreasonable exactions and inexcusable violence, their cries of "Give!" "Give!" never to be satisfied, excited the Liberals, in both countries, to reprisals. In Switzerland the true Republicans took up arms simply to re-establish their brethren, the Unionists, within the territories of the traitorous alliance, in the possessions of those privileges which had been ravished from them by force. In the same manner the American Republicans responded to the Federal call to re-establish a violated Constitution. If, in order to do so, they were compelled to break the fetters of the Slave, what right had the chattel-owners to complain? Had they not trampled and spat upon the very compact which protected them in their unrighteous tyranny; their hold upon the bodies and souls of their fellow men.

As hereinbefore mentioned the Treaty of Alliance constituting the 𝕾𝖔𝖓𝖉𝖊𝖗𝖇𝖚𝖓𝖉 (SECESSION Compact or Sep-

arate LEAGUE of UR SCHWYZ, Old or Primitive Switzerland,) was made public at FREYBURG in May, 1846. In
June it was, as it were, officially promulgated.

Nothing new however was published, for Swiss Treason,
like Southern Secession, had not been deliberated in se-
cret. The very publicity of its proceedings and threats
led the majority to suppose that there was more in them
of menace than intention. Practical men could not believe that Cantons or States would sacrifice their interests
to their passions.'

Honest and sober men, however, both in Switzerland
and in this country, were woefully mistaken.

Even as Secession arrayed ELEVEN SLAVEHOLDING
STATES, and relied with certainty on the co-operation of
THREE more to resist the efforts of the Union abiding
nineteen Free States, the Sonderbund arrayed seven Seceding Cantons against twelve Cantons and two Half-
Cantons faithful to the Constitution. One Canton and
two Half-Cantons, like our doubting or doubtful Border
States, remained indifferent, and constituted what has
been styled the "Neutral Sonderbund." The effect of
their attitude was like that of a cold palsy, upon many
in the loyal districts who occupied about the same unin-
teresting position as the Anti-coercion Unionists among
us. One Canton, the money-making city of Basle, was
deterred from decided action by fears of trade, but the
Basle country, like rural New York, was true as steel to
the Constitution and Union.

It may be interesting to consider the relative position
and forces of the two camps into which Switzerland was
decided.

Here was a little free country containing less than
2,400,000 inhabitants, all told, surrounded by mighty

sovereignties sympathising with, and aiding, the revolutionists, menaced by an internal convulsion, which arrayed 116,000 people, disposed in natural fortresses of prodigious strength and susceptible of protracted resistance, against 1,830,000 faithful subjects and about 111,000 neutrals. The proportion was LIBERALS, FEDERALISTS or UNIONISTS, *eighteen*, to Ultramontanists, Sonderbundists or Rebels, *five*, to *Neutrals*, *one*. The relative numbers in our own case are about the same, throwing out the slave element, Loyalists or Unionists, *nineteen and one-fourth*, Slavocrats, Secessionsts or Rebels, *five*, Neutrals, *three*.— Our Rebels however have this advantage, that their Slaves are a source of Strength, and the Sympathy of our Copperheads or Peace party almost divided our forces.

The relative area of loyal and rebel territory were in both cases not much unlike. The territory of the Swiss Secession Cantons was, it is true, much more dislocated than that of the Confederate States, but its actual susceptibility of defence was not inferior. The Districts of the Separate League lay in a crescent shape, somewhat resembling one of the mediæval hunting horns, with a very large bell and mouth-piece. The latter, to the West, rested upon the Lake of NEUCHATEL, while the LAKE of the FOUR CANTONS not inaptly represented the orifice of the former. The SONDERBUND (Secession League) certainly enjoyed the best position militarily considered, for their troops could operate on interior lines while the Federals, as in our own case, were obliged to move on difficult exterior lines.

What is more, just as the Secessionists had the pick, as they supposed, of our West Point officers, the Swiss Rebels had the advantage of entrusting their commands to leaders of great experience who had witnessed and participated in the operations of actual war upon a large scale. Many of these officers were the more devoted to the Ultramontane party, and the more bitterly opposed the Liberals, from the fact that their talents had been exercised in the service of the king of Naples and other despotic monarchs, where their superior abilities, Swiss courage, and the confidence, which their national character justified, had given them opportunities far beyond those commensurate with their actual rank. Foreign officers also joined this unholy league.

These coincidences could be followed out much further would time permit, but one point remains to be noticed. While the Ultramontanists, like the Slave faction, Secessionists and Copperheads, were claiming the most unrestricted liberty for themselves, their tyranny exceeded all bounds, They abolished the Liberty of the Press, and permitted just as much free speech as would furnish an excuse for the punishment of the speaker. PESTALOZZI, the celebrated Swiss " St. Vincent de Paul of Education," furnishes the only excuse for the excesses of the Separate League Cantons. " He saw that the principal CAUSE of the misery of the multitude was their IGNORANCE, which did not allow them to make use of their political rights, even for the amelioration of their position." The same can be the only explanation for the action and atrocities of the Rebels. Moreover had our Rebels been less ignorant, they would not have permitted themselves to be slaughtered and expended for the interests of a wicked oligarchy.

In the month of May, 1846. as we have said, the treaty of disunion constituting the *Sonderbund* (Separate League or Secession-Union) of Ur-Schweiz (the Switzerland of old time) was published.

Nothing new, however, was promulgated, for just as treason at the South has been germinating for thirty years, so the Sonderbund doctrine was completely systematized some time before the first attack was made upon the Swiss secessionists by the liberals.

Nine months of conciliatory negotiation elapsed before the Swiss Diet came to the decision to act by force of arms. During that time the constitutional party was gradually becoming more and more satisfied that nothing remained but a resort to the "*ultima ratio regum*." The attitude of the Sonderbundists discovered that all other reasoning was in vain. Much the same state of things existed in the secession cantons as now exists in the seceding states. There, as here, there was a minority Union party who made themselves heard. There, as here, they attempted to make themselves felt also, but, "whelmed in blood and tears," they were trampled under foot with savage severity by a treasonable majority. The Unionists at Lucerne and in other seceding cantons, experienced exactly what would be the fate of a conservative minority in Charleston, exactly what has been the fate of such a minority in Tennessee. They were either bayoneted, or crushed by legal prosecution, into silence.

The Rebel Swiss ought to have fought well. They were fanatics in the closest application of the word, and of a race brave, under any circumstances, to a proverb. They had sharpened their swords on the tomb of the martyred St. Maurice, their rifles had been solemnly blessed by their spiritual guides, visions and miracles had been reported to cheer their hopes, and human assistance from abroad, and supernatural intervention from above, were confidently expected.

Spiritual avarice, if the term be admissable, lent that vigor to the Sonderbund that the thirst for material wealth, borrowing the mantle of chivalry, had infused into the lords and champions of Cottondom.

Slowly but surely the unionist cantons proceeded with their preparations. On the 20th of July, 1847, the conservative portion of the Diet declared the Sonderbund, or Separate League, dissolved, and by successive decrees 11th August and 3d September, proceeded to forbid the introduction of arms into the revolted states, and finally 20th–29th October, to organize its forces for definitive action. In other words, the loyal and true cantons made ready to enforce the laws and coerce the rebels into submission.

Then MEYER, deputy of Lucerne, in behalf of the Sonderbund-Seven, rose in the Federal Diet and said "The moment has come for us to withdraw." Invoking God's name, he cast upon the Federal, Loyal or Union representatives all present and future responsibility for coming events. Then the Rebel deputies departed. Had our Arch-rebel DAVIS and his associates critically studied the conduct of the Swiss secession leaders, they could not have imitated and repeated with more hypocritical solemnity the farce of an unvoluntary departure—a withdrawing, a sundering, a Secession, deliberately planned and long since resolved upon, which was to plunge a peaceful, prosperous people in flames, in blood and in tears.

The Swiss Sonderbund Campaign.

The political difficulties in Switzerland had now reached their climax. The analogous period of our own struggle was the time of President Lincoln's inauguration. To use the quaint but emphatic old English phraseology, Loyalty and Disloyalty looked one another in the face. Both parties felt that the question, now, could not be determined without bloodshed. The Federal Diet might, with reason, have addressed to the Rebel Administrative Council, the words of King JOHN to the French monarch, before the walls of Angiers:

> Peace be to France; if France in peace permit
> Our just and lineal entrance to our own!
> If not; bleed France, and peace ascend to heaven!
> While's we. God's wrathful agent, do correct
> Their proud contempt that beat His peace to heaven.

These sentiments of England's King convey the very gist of Lincoln's inaugural. What a difference, however, between the immediate consequents of the declaration of the Swiss Federal Diet and those of the Presidential Address.

The first Swiss Federal Call for Volunteers was for 50,000 men, equal in proportion to our population to a levy of 550,000. President LINCOLN's first demand was for 75,000 men, equal in proportion to the *Swiss population to less than* 7,000.

This was the GREAT MISTAKE of our War.

The second Swiss Federal Call was for 90,000 men, equivalent in the United States to a levy of 1,000,000; 100,000 responded.

Literally,—

> "The drum was beat; and lo!
> The plough, the work-shop is forsaken, all
> *Swarm* to the old, familiar, long-loved banner."

and bound upon their left arms, above the elbow, the red band, emblazoned with the white Helvetian cross, the symbol of National or Federal service. This Armlet is a token that the Militiaman is no longer at the disposition of the individual Canton or State, to which he belongs, but of the whole Confederation or Union.

On the mountains and in the valleys, in the marts and in the manufactories of every loyal territory, the cry " To

Arms! the country is in danger!" was universal. Everywhere men felt and acted up to the sentiment.

> " Ever constant, ever true,
> Let the Word be No SURRENDER !
> Boldly dare, and greatly do:
> This shall bring us greatly through:
> No SURRENDER ! No SURRENDER !"

On the 26th October, 1847, General DUFOUR, of Geneva,
the Federal Commander-in-Chief, issued his proclamation
to an Army of from 90,000 to 100,000 confederated free-
men, formed into six divisions, with two hundred and
sixty pieces of artillery. To these the Secession party
opposed 30,000, in Lucerne, besides an army corps in other
districts, and multitudes of mere militia filled with ra-
ging enthusiasm. The bloodthirstiness evinced long
beforehand by the Ultras of the Sonderbund was horrible,
as repugnant to civilization as that of the majority of our
Secessionists. "All means were employed to excite fanaticism. The Papal Nuncio himself blessed the banners
of those going to the frontiers, as formerly before the fra-
tricidal war of Villmergen. Jesuits were appointed field-
chaplains. Blessed amulets were distributed to the hordes
of the Landsturm, to protect them from shot and sword,
and preachers from the pulpit assured all the people of
the assistance of the Virgin Mary to preserve them from
death and make their victory sure."

The regularly organized forces of the Sonderbund have
been estimated as high as 36,000, supported by a *Landsturm* of 48,000. Total disposable numbers 83,000. From
a comparison of all the different statements, between regularly organized troops, militia proper, &c., out of a population of 2,400,000, at least 200,000 must have been in
the field, or in garrison, or doing duty with the armies in
the opposing camps. This would be equivalent to 2,250,

000 out of the population of our whole country, North and South.

It may seem surprising that a comparatively poor country like Switzerland could set in motion so large an army at so short a notice. The explanation is clear and convincing. The Cantons possess a Militia so admirably organized that it can be placed on a war footing at once. The Swiss motto is one which should be ours, *"no Regular Army but every Citizen a Soldier."* Our constitution contemplated this result. The Swiss Federal triumph was undoubtedly due to this *preparation for* WAR *in time of* PEACE.

Dufour's address, " as energetic as it was moderate," seemed like the signal of the prompter for the rolling up of the curtain. Through what a series of magnificent scenery, rolled on the vigorous action of the short but startling, stringent but splendid, drama of Swiss military coercion.

Strong in the Righteousness of their cause, the Loyal columns marched out from their homes to extinguish Secession. Moving proudly on, battery to battery, squadron to squadron, battalion to battalion answered with,—

"A martial song like a trumpet's call."

From street and door-step, window and house top, hill and valley, matrons and maids, and all incapable of bearing arms, echoed encouragement.—

"Singing of men that in battle array,
Ready in heart and ready in hand,
March with banner and bugle and fife,
To the Death for their Native Land."

"Singing of Death, and of honor that cannot die"— Death or the Salvation of the Fatherland.

General WILLIAM HENRY DUFOUR, the Crusher of the Souderbund, like our MEADE, the Hero of Gettysburgh, was not by birth a Swiss. Even as MEADE was born at Cadiz, in Spain, the son of Pennsylvanian parents, even so DUFOUR, although born at *Constance*, in *Baden*, sprang from a family natives of *Geneva*. In the latter city he received his early education and made mathematics his peculiar study. When Geneva had been incorporated with France, he entered in 1807, the Polytechnic school at Paris, and, in 1809, received his first commission in the corps of military Engineers.*

To this peculiarly scientific branch of the service we owe several of our best Generals, such as ROSECRANS, GILLMORE, MEADE, if a combination not a speciality of talent is the test of superiority.

At the period Dufour was appointed Commander-in-Chief, he had attained the age of 60 years. In personal appearance, if his portrait exposed for sale at the time, is reliable, he closely resembled, in face and form, our illustrious and lamented Clay, nor did he yield to that

---

* DUFOUR participated in the last campaigns of the Empire, and rose to the rank of Captain. After the fall of Napoleon he entered the Swiss Federal Service, and soon became Colonel, the highest recognized grade. In 1831, he was appointed Chief of the General Staff, and a short time afterwards Quartermaster-General.— To him was confided the Direction of the Triangulation, the basis of the Topographical map of Switzerland. As Chief Instructor of Engineering at the Federal Military School at Thun, he rendered important services to his country. In 1840, he published his "*Memoir on the Artillery of Antiquity and of the Middle Ages*," and, in 1842, his "*Manual of* TACTICS *for Officers of* ALL ARMS," one of the best works of the kind in existence. In 1847, DUFOUR, at the age of 60, received, with the title of General, the command of the Army opposed to the SONDERBUND. "*His skillful manœuvres speedily insured the Triumph of Liberal Switzerland. Forestalled by the rapidity of his action, foreign governments did not dare to interfere, and the Roman Catholics sued for pardon. This* CAMPAIGN *preserved the* UNITY *and, perhaps, the* INDEPENDENCE *of the* HELVETIAN CONFEDERATION." It won for General DUFOUR numerous testimonials of National gratitude. The Federal Diet voted him a Sabre of Honor and a Donative of ($8,000) 40,000 francs, (*Dict : des Contemporains.*) Since this triumphant proof of his ability, DUFOUR has been employed in a number of diplomatic missions, secret as well as public, in all of which he acquired as much credit and respect as in his military operations. DUFOUR is Grand Officer of the French Legion of Honor.

noble exponent of loyal sentiments in the boldness, purity and self-negation of his patriotism.

"On the 4th November, 1847, a decree of the Diet ordered General Dufour to dissolve the Sonderbund by force of arms." "Now the statesmen had done their part; the sword must give the fatal blow." It was found difficult to bring such numerous battalions into the field and pay and feed them, at a time when Switzerland was still suffering from the effects of a year of scarcity and pecuniary embarrassments; but the admirable energy of Berne, the metropolis, provided all. That canton had already imposed on itself all kinds of sacrifices. It had already emptied its treasury and its arsenals, yet it did not hesitate to lend half a million of Swiss francs to the confederation; proving that it was still worthy of the glorious days of its War of Independence.

Even the Progress of Hostilities in SWITZERLAND bears out the Analogy to the present War in the UNITED STATES. Just as the first attack was made upon our Federal Troops, constituting the Garrisons of Forts SUM-TER and PICKENS, on our Eastern and South Eastern maritime frontier, before the idea of Coercion was fully inaugurated, just so attempts were made to resist the Federal authorities in the extreme Northern and North Eastern Cantons of AARGAU and ST. GALL. Both these partial insurrections, happily, had the same result as our Rebels attempt upon SANTA ROSA Island, opposite Pensacola. They were quickly suppressed. Nor was the first attack upon our Federal troops, stationed at the extreme South-western posts of the Union, in TEXAS, without a parallel abroad. Just so, before the Swiss national army was fully arrayed, the Sonderbund faction transported a body of Uranians, troops of Uri, with great difficulty, across the Lepontian Alps, and made an attack upon the

Federals in the outlying Canton of Ticino, which projects southwards like a cape, into Lombardy. The first result however in the Tessinese was the exact reverse of that in Texas, since two of the Sonderbundist leaders paid for their temerity with their lives. The Loyal Swiss had a Lyon there, just as we had when most needed, in Missouri, —Colonel, Lutini. Happier than our lamented soldier-martyr, he survived the war to wear the laurels he had nobly won in defending the integrity of his country. This affair occurred on the southern slope of the *St. Gothard,* famous for the transit of Suwarrow in 1800. Thus blood had been shed by the rebels, on the very day that the Proclamation was issued for the Suppression of the Separate League, by force of arms.

Dufour's plan of operations was founded on the very Anaconda System which has lately been so much decried and even derided in this country. It was successful. He surrounded the territories of the Sonderbund with an immense chain of troops, closing every entrance and exit. Simultaneously, he threw a separate coil around the Canton of Freyburg, partly detached from its confederate sisters. At the same time he struck with the instinctive energy of genius at one of the vital points of the rebellion. Like the keen Lammergeyer of the Alps, amid whose embattled ranges he was operating, with huge expanded wings feathered with steel, he swooped down on his quarry, Freyburg. To borrow the language of the gentle sport of Falconry, "unhooded and thrown off, his stoop" was like the levin-bolt, direct and dazzling, unimpeded by the "jesses" of red tape, untrammelled by the electric "signals" of beaurocratic interference. The matured vigor of Dufour's "Forwards" strategy recalls the vivid comparison of Octavio Piccolomini

"Straight forward goes the Lightning's,
Straight forward goes the cannon-ball's fearful path,
Swift, by directest course, It hurtles on,
Shattering It makes Its way, that It may shatter."

The Federal Diet, as soon as it had appealed to arms,
committed everything to the grey-haired general to whom
they had entrusted the Sword. This was as it should have
been, and the result justified their confidence. The members of the Diet felt the influence of, the Federal Military
School of Thun, the "West Point" of the Swiss Confederation. The French Emperor Louis Napoleon was a
pupil of this institution. There he had made his debut
in the Artillery, just as his uncle had graduated at
Brienne, to enter the same Arm of the French service. Others had seen service themselves. All the Members of
Diet had the sufficient judgment to appreciate and con-
cede, that

" In the Field,
There, must the PRESENT ONE direct, Supreme,
The Head in Person rule ; his *own* eye see.—
If War-Chief needs all Nature's greatest gifts,
Grudge him not then, to live in all the vast
Proportions of her greatness. He, alone,
The living oracle, indwelling, must consult
Not orders old, dead books, or musty papers."

Nor had the Swiss general, himself forgotten the ADAGE
of the Great Captain under whose eagles he had made his
first campaigns, that " *he, who gropes* (or moves irresolute-
ly) *loses*." He knew that at this crisis, to "amuse himself at Gembloux" would ruin his country. Dufour was
imbued with the spirit of those hero-bards evoked by the
War of 1812-'13, for the Deliverance of Germany, whose
poetic gems like

" Sparks of noble spirits flew,"

struck out by the clash between Tyranny and Avenging
Freedom. A wonderful generation that of KORNER, brothers. in race and instincts, of ZWINGLI, they poured forth

their blood and their song with equal courage and fire for
their country. Sword in hand, the minstrel-martyr thundered the vital question :—

> "WHAT would the Singer's Fatherland?—
> Strike to her feet the servile race,
> Forth, from her soil, the bloodhound chase,
> FREE, *bear* FREE SONS (upon her face)
> Or bed them, FREE, beneath her sand ;
> THAT would my Fatherland !

And, in trumpet tones KORNER responded, a few hours
before he fell upon the field of Gadebush, singing his
Sword-Song while the wing of the death-angel beat
chilly upon him :—

> "What rapture thus to be
> The Guardian of the Free.
> Hurrah !"

Such were the Germans of 1812-'15 under BLUCHER ;
such were the Swiss of 1847, under DUFOUR, who proved

> "SKILL, *mixed with* WILL, *is he that teaches best.*"

DUFOUR doubtless determined to commence his active
operations with the capture of Freyburg, for several
reasons: *morally*, because it had long been a centre
of Ultramontane intrigue and Secession conspiracies ;
physically, because the season was late for campaigning
in a mountain region, and neither politics nor strategy
could permit any unnecessary delay ; *militarily*, because
it lay separate and unsupported. He selected FREYBURG
just as a good General falls unexpectedly on a dislocated
corps or division *en aire*. The result showed that Dufour's
plans had been digested with consummate discretion.

The Canton of Freyburg is very peculiarly situated.
Its capital, Dufour's object, even more so. Although
completely embraced by the Liberal Cantons of Berne
and Vaud, it has always been noted for its intolerance.
Bisected by the Saane, or Sarine, the southern half is

mountainous but rich in pastures, while the northern embraces some of the finest agricultural ground in Switzerland. Portions of the latter are said to resemble districts in England, pleasant to the eyes of the farmer. Moreover this northern district is one of the few of the Confederation which produces corn in sufficient quantities to render it independent of foreign supplies. Between its animal and vegetable productions, the Canton is self-sustaining. Consequently as the harvest had been gathered, it should have made a protracted defence.

Three languages are spoken in this Canton. Notwithstanding, the feelings of the people were not divided as a rule, for the proportion of Protestants is very small and generally confined to particular localities. French is the predominating dialect towards the North, West, and in the towns, German in the North-east, and Romansch, a corruption of the Latin, in the South.

> "A Babylonish dialect,
> Which learned pedants much affect;
> It was a parti-colored dress
> Of patch'd and piebald languages."

The capital is even more singular, physically, morally, and relatively, than the canton. The upper town is French, the lower is German, both were behind the times, exclusive, opposed to new men and new ideas. SIMOND says "this town is so exactly on the limits of the Gallic and Germanic idioms, that one half of the inhabitants do not understand the other." Its site resembles that of Constantine in Algeria; Civita Castellana in Viterbo, States of the Church; and Vicksburgh. Just as the two former are seated on scarped rocks and the latter on a bluff, in Ox-bows of the Oued-el-Kebir, Rio Maggiore and the Mississippi, just so Freyburg is situated on an elevated tongue of soft sand-stone rock, perforated with caverns, and bare of vegetation, washed on three sides by the turbid Saane,

flowing without beauty, in its profound gloomy chasm.
Before it, to the north, stretches as stated, one of the
finest agricultural districts in the XXII Cantons. Behind
it tower the Bernese Alps and mountain citadels of the
Valais. With the latter it is connected by only a single
good road, while five grand routes diverge from its gates
to Berne, the Lakes of Bienne, Morat, Neuchatel and
Geneva. The territory embraced between them, resembles
a Fan, of which the Roads represent the Ribs, having a
radius of fifteen miles. Of this fan, Freyburg city constitutes the knob or handle, grasped by the rapid Saane,
rushing around and beneath the town, overhung by
quaint buildings which seem to need only a gust of wind
to topple them over the precipice into the gulf below. It
is strange that while thus united, to the east, north and
west with the land of Progress and Liberality, by easy
and fine roads and, to the south, the citadel of Romanism
by only one circuitous route, Freyburg has lain buried in
the sleep of apathy or worse. The population seemed
willing to receive nothing beneficial by the many channels
from the north, and any amount of prejudicial influences
through the single one to the rear. They admitted they
were behind the time, but consoled themselves that other
Romanist Swiss were still more so. They were now
destined to realize the truth of Victor Hugo's remark
that "the North and the People are the reservoirs of
humanity."

"Yet, FREEDOM! yet thy banner, torn, but flying,
Streams like a thunder-storm against the wind:
Thy trumpet voice tho' broken now and dying,
The loudest still the tempest leaves behind;
Thy tree hath lost its blossoms, and the rind
Chopp'd by the axe seems rough and little worth,
But the sap lasts,—and still the seed we find
Sown deep, *even in the bosom of the* NORTH ;
So shall a better spring less bitter fruit bring forth."

Seated aloft and looking out in every direction

upon scenery unexceeded in beauty and sublimity, in
full view of the majestic Alps, the birthplace of the
Freyburgher resembles, in its glorious elevation and sur-
roundings, the cradle of Zwingli. Notwithstanding, the
former seemed to have derived therefrom ideas diametri-
cally opposite to the celestial influences which nature
infused into the expanding mind of the Reformer of
Zurich. Prior to its capture by Dufour, in 1847, it was
the stronghold of the Roman Catholic priesthood. Previous to that date the education of its population had
been in the hands of the Jesuits, and their College in this
city had been the chief nursery of the Society out of Italy.
This may account for the fact, that down to 1782, the
government of Zurich was the closest aristocracy or oligarchy, even among those Cantons whose people in " the
middle ages, vegetated under the cudgels of their lords
and the crosiers of their bishops." In the administration
of its public affairs, it was styled the Venice of Switzerland. Nor does the comparison between Freyburg and
the Queen of the Adriatic cease with the consideration
of its government. Just as the latter is almost unique in
its peculiar natural position, architecture and other objects
of curiosity, just so Freyburg greets the curious traveller
with an unwonted display of mediæval constructions and
feudal remains. "The dirt, the Madonnas, the colossal
crucifixes, strongly recalled Italy." "Striking and romantic," and "possessing so many attributes of the pictur-
esque" it has an exterior " with which the meanness
of the interior does not correspond." "Even in these days
(1841) it contained five convents for men and four for
women, within its walls. One of these is a college, on
a very large scale, ' a staring, modern building, like a
manufactory, with five stories,' for the Jesuits." "On
the whole, the place is like no other in Switzerland."

Long lines of embattled walls climb its steep heights
and plunge into the gloom of the Sarine. Watch-towers
shoot up from space to space, and mediæval bastions defend its gates, specimens of the first steps of scientific
engineering. The massive constructions might almost
laugh to scorn a siege undertaken with the ordinary
field artillery of sixteen years since, and would have
done so had the spirit of Freyburg's men equalled the
solidity of its walls.

'It has been remarked that Dufour's plan of operations
had been digested with consummate discretion. It was
now carried out with equal ability.

The chief command of the Secessionists in this district,
had been confided to Gen. MAILLARDOZ. This officer had
served with distinction under the same master in the Art
of War, Napoleon, as DUFOUR; likewise under the Bour-
bon Restoration in France. Yet how inferior did he
prove himself in the application of the rules, learned
under the same ensigns. Dufour completely outwitted
him. Maillardoz had been led to expect that he would
be attacked from the east. He anticipated that the principal forces of the Confederation would invade Freyburg
by Laupen, the scene of a wonderful victory of the republican Bernese over the league of the imperialist Nobles,
in 1339,—Neuencck, and Schwarzenburg, all three on
the river Sense, the boundary between the cantons of
Berne and Freyburg. From that quarter patriotic Ochsenbein, who commanded the Free Corps, which had
been beaten back from Lucerne in 1845, was indeed
advancing. This movement, however, was more to
attract the attention of the Rebel General than intended
as a real attack, although capable, if necessary, of becoming one. Ochsenbein's march of about 18 miles, had to

be made through long, deep and narrow defiles, susceptible of murderous defence, by the main route from Berne to Freyburg. This road emerging from the Bear's Gate of the Capital of the Confederation, passes through a difficult but magnificent country, crosses the Sarine by a splendid suspension bridge 941 feet long, at an elevation of 180 feet, and delivers the traveller, at once, by a breach through the old houses, in the very heart of Freyburg. Previous to the erection of this bridge, it required an hour of difficult descent, detour, and ascent, to cross the gorge of the Sarine, which is now accomplished in two minutes.

While thus the attention of the Freyburghers was fascinated by the approach of Ochsenbein from the East, the other Federal divisions had been massed to the northward, in the loyal district of Morat, and, to the westward, in the Canton of Vaud, which sweeps round, beyond the head of the lakes of Geneva, to St. Maurice on the Road to Sion. On the 9th and 10th November, five days after promulgation of the Decree of the Federal Diet for the forcible dissolution of the Sonderbund, twenty thousand loyal troops invaded Freyburg. Relatively, this Canton occupied the same position in regard to the Sonderbund League that Virginia held to our own Rebel Confederacy. The frontier towns were occupied without a shot being fired. The capture of Staffis or Estavayer, on the Lake of Neuchatel, presents a perfect parallel to the capture of Alexandria on the Potomac. The Federals were astonished to meet with no opposition. This was the more surprising since the whole canton of Freyburg, the district of the capital city especially, was strongly defended by nature and art. This simultaneous closing in, would be exactly exemplified by the act of pushing in one of those Fans, whose size can be reduced, at once, one half, by their ribs shutting into themselves like the joints of a telescope. From the north and west, strong columns advanced upon four of the five roads which come together at Freyburg. The 1st, most easterly, the direct connection between the beleaguered town and nucleus or main body of the Sonderbund, was already closed by Ochsenbein's occupation of Neueneck. The positions of Morat and Estavayer, on the 2d and 3d, now precluded all access to the lakes of Bienne and Neuchatel, by which the Rebels hoped to receive supplies from France, as well as smuggled assistance from "Copperhead" Neuchatel itself. The capture of Romont, on the 4th, and Chatel St. Denis, on the 5th, road, cut off all hopes of aid from sympathizing Savoy, across the lake of Geneva, through traitors in Lausanne and Vevay. Finally, the occupation of Bulle, at the junction of the road to Vevay, the 5th, and the main route to the Valais, severed that, the last source of supply. From Bulle, likewise, the mountain road through the same valley, but on the opposite shore, of the Sarine, could be completely supervised and commanded. On the 11th November, the Federals resumed their advance and, driving the rebels before them, huddled them in upon a centre incapable, under the circumstances, of maintaining such numbers. On the morning of the 12th November, Freyburg found itself completely surrounded on the west or left side of the Sarine, by an army of upwards of twenty thousand men, ready to move to the assault. Ochsenbein's division, meanwhile, observed the other side. Completely isolated. Freyburg had now to make good its boasts, and stand or fall alone.

The population of this capital were commanded by officers considered skillful, and had themselves a good

military reputation. "It was announced in foreign countries that the Catholics of Freyburg would renew the
wonders of the heroic defence of Saragossa." The natural position of the Spanish city was by no means as
strong. All that was required was a like determination
in the people. This did not exist and, before a shot was
fired, the mere sight of the environing masses had engendered ideas of submission. From his headquarters at
Avenches, about six miles to the north, on the 12th,
Dufour had addressed a proclamation to his army and on
the 13th, had despatched a flag of truce to the authorities
of the beleaguered town to convince them of the futility
of defence. The Council of State convoked a Council of
War, and the latter were sufficiently intimidated at the
aspect of affairs to request a suspension of arms. This
was granted, conditionally, till the morning of the 14th.
Meanwhile the Federal Colonel Rilliet, commanding the
1st Division of Dufour's army, was either ignorant of this
armistice or unwilling to accept it, unless his troops were
permitted to occupy the Wood of Dailliettes. This wood
appears to have been the key-point of the Freyburgher's
line of defence, on the North of the Sarine. It had been
fortified with care and occupied by eleven hundred Rebels, with orders to hold it to the last man. Rilliet's summons to evacuate this post was refused. This was on
the evening of the 13th. Thereupon the works were
attacked, and the fiery Liberals of Vaud carried the main
redoubts of Bertigny. The fighting continued after night-
fall. Amid the darkness the Vaud troops charged
through the abatis and ditches and drove the Freyburgher's out of the wood. Had daylight lasted another
hour, the Federals would have taken the City by storm.
The struggle had been fierce and bloody, but it rendered
farther sacrifices needless. The Inspiration of Liberty

proved too powerful even for the Fanaticism of a Religious Education, whose cardinal principle is blind and absolute obedience. At 8 A. M., on the 14th, Freyburg capitulated and withdrew from the Sonderbund.

General MAILLARDOZ, the rebel commander, was obliged to seek refuge in the Federal headquarters against the outrages of his own troops, furious at their defeat, which they attributed to him while due to their own feeble resistance. Accused of betraying his associates in treason, he subsequently died in obscurity and misery. The Jesuits were expelled, the Canton militarily occupied and thoroughly subjugated, and, amid tears of joy, the incarceratsd Unionists welcomed their deliverers. To carry out the comparison in our own case, witness the reception of BURNSIDE in Eastern Tennessee. Thus satisfactorily the curtain fell on the first act of the Grand Drama of Coercion. Its action embraced a period of six days.

Meanwhile, despite the loyal successes and their own disparity of forces, the Rebels were enabled to make incursions into Loyal Cantons bordering on their own territory. just as Maryland and Pennsylvania have suffered from Rebel invasion, and Ohio from Secessionist inroads. The efforts of the Swiss Sonderbundists, however, were repelled and chastised with a celerity and loss which did not occur in our own country.

The fall of Freyburg did not make a decided impression on the more violent partisans of the Separate League.— "Matters would be very different," they said, "in Lucerne and in the Primitive Cantons." "The Sonderbund General DI SALIS SOGLIO had at his disposal 30.000 men, at present entrenched behind impregnable positions. With such advantages he would be able," it was added, "to arrest for years the progress of General Dufour's 60,000 men." Lucerne was still proud of its victory over the "Free Companions" or Free Corps, in 1844 and 1845, and as for the Forest States, they were set down as unconquerable. A slight success gained at Dietwyl, in Argovia, on the 10th November, by the Secessionist forces of Schwytz had confirmed all these hopes. Nevertheless, on the 20th November, Zug, the Georgia, as to location, of the Sonderbund, "terrified by the very appearance of the Federal flag, and somewhat lukewarm moreover, in the cause of rebellion, offered to capitulate, and on the 21st abandoned the Sonderbund. This alarmed even the most ardent *Fire-eaters* at the very headquarters of resistance to law, although the discouraging intelligence reached Lucerne at the very moment when the Imperialist Prince Schwartzenberg was tendering his sword to the Ultramontane League, to which Austria had renewed her promises of pecuniary aid and other assistance. The opportune submission of Zug was doubly satisfactory. Its people received the Federals with rejoicing, and relieved them from the danger of a flank attack, not only throughout their advance, but at the very moment of their collision with the enemy. What is more, it enabled the Federals to completely turn the strongest works upon which the safety of Lucerne depended. It likewise obviated delay almost as dangerous to the Loyal party as a check or partial defeat, for the leaders of the Sonderbund had positive assurances of foreign intervention in their favor, if they only could hold out a few days longer.

In the selection of their leaders both the Loyal and Rebel Swiss presented a marked contrast to the action of our own people, whose infatuation leads them, too often, to entrust the direction of military affairs to civilians of little or no experience in such matters.

Another error into which we have fallen is the idea

that young officers are, *per se*, superior to old officers, because a few examples of precocious generalship have startled the world. People forget that Alexander, Gustavus, Frederic, and even Napoleon, were surrounded by experienced officers of the highest merit, and a veteran or excellent soldiery. DUFOUR, as was stated, was sixty. His opponent, DI SALIS-SOGLIO, was fifty seven. He belonged to the old aristocratic SALIS family, which even down to the year of his birth 1790, ruled alone, like sovereigns, in the democratic Grisons, with an influence indirectly absolute. He had served with distinction against Napoleon, so that he and Dufour commenced and ended their careers in opposing camps. Morally, however, each had changed sides. In 1813-'14, di Salis-Soglio was fighting for the Liberation of Germany from the curse of a tyranny, which Dufour, and this latter's defeated antagonist, Maillardoz were assisting to maintain. In 1847, di Salis-Soglio, although a Protestant, was commanding in behalf of the Jesuits, while Dufour was the champion of Free Thought and Liberty in general. It has been remarked that in the Swiss conflicts since the XVI century, the pedantic Protestants and the Jesuits, for their own interests, always joined hands with the Foreign Powers against the Liberals. Ochsenbein, aged thirty six, must have been a man of more than ordinary ability. He had been chief of the Federal Staff, President of the Berne Cantonal Administration, and, through that position, Presiding Officer of the Federal Diet. Afterwards he was a general in the service of Napoleon III. The other Division commanders justified the confidence of the nation.

After the conquest of Freyburg, DUFOUR's next great object was the capture of LUCERNE. Even there, despite the apparent unanimity of Rebel sentiment, an element of loyalty existed, suppressed however with the greatest severity. Moreover, while the Federal columns were concentrating for decisive action, many of the necessaries of life were already wanting in the main Rebel stronghold. Dufour now displayed as much Practical Strategy in his movements against this hot bed of seditition, as he had shown in his previous operations. Nor was the Swiss Federal Secretary of State less equal to his position than the gray-haired General.in-Chief. His course was the direct opposite of that pursued by our own high official in the same relative position. He would not allow the French Embassy to communicate with the traitor authorities in Lucerne, or afford any moral support to the Rebel main-army, strangling in the coil of the loyal Anaconda.

On the 16th November, Dufour transferred his headquarters to AARAU. This town lies on the Aar, about thirty miles N, N. W. of Lucerne. It is situated at the apex of an ellipse, whose butt is marked out by the curve of the Emme and Reuss. Opposite the centre of this convex, stands LUCERNE, at the foot of the lake of the Four Cantons. It is useless in this connection, to go into a detailed description of this city. It was the residence of the Papal Nuncio; since 1845 one of the headquarters of the Jesuits; contained, according to Murray, a population of eight thousand one hundred and fifty-nine Roman Catholics and one hundred and eighty Protestants; and had distinguished itself, during the two preceding years, by the persecution of its citizens opposed to the majority or dominant party. Of these prosecutions Zschokke remarks "No page in the history of Switzerland is stained with blacker sins in the administration of public justice." Lucerne not only resembled Charleston in the ultra-intolerance of its institutions but likewise in its military position. Just as that stronghold of Slavery, Nullification and Secession was formerly extremely defensible in itself, just so this centre of Ultramontanism or spiritual Serfdom and Sonderbundism was, a century since, a place of military importance, Even as the South Carolinian metropolis triumphantly repulsed a British attack in 1776, and was only captured after a sharp siege by Sir Henry Clinton in 1780; so the Swiss citadel, centre or pivot of the successive "Separate Leagues" had held its enemies at bay with its circle of massive feudal watch-towers, gothic battlements and walls. Both are no longer tenable in these days of improved artillery after their advanced works have fallen. Lucerne demonstrated and Charleston is now exemplifying that their safety depends on the maintenance of an exterior line of great natural strength. This line of defence, a little concave towards the Swiss town constitutes the shortest diameter of the egg-shaped district embraced within the most eastern and western of the five main roads, diverging from Aarau and converging to Lucerne, which band it like meridian lines. The principal positions which protect Lucerne, together, form a flattened arc having a chord of twenty-two miles. Of this the eastern extremity rests on the lake of Zug and the western on the town of Willisau, on the Wigger, while its centre touches the southern extremity of the Lake of Sempach.

The Federal main army whose headquarters were at Aarau was distributed into four grand divisions, to break, with a simultaneous shock, through this line of formidable positions from the North. A column of the first, most easterly, army-corps so to speak advanced through the extreme eastern portion of Aargau, which thrusts itself South, far down, between the Cantons of Zug and Argovia. This district is known in Switzerland as the FREIAMT, or Free Bailiwicks. Prior to 1814, it had been a bone of contention, on a question of jurisdiction, between Zug and Argovia. Subsequent to that date, it proved an apple of discord in the Federal Diet. The Suppression of the Monastical institutions therein, for treasonable practices and violence against the established authorities, led, ostensibly, to the formation of the Sonderbund in 1843–'6–'7. As this district is flanked for about half its depth, by the territory of Zug, it was fortunate for the Federals that this Rebel Canton had submitted to them. Already a large portion of it had been militarily occupied by Union troops. The second column of the first corps, or Division-ZIEGLER, followed the 3d road, along the stream of the Winen, midway between the Hallwyler and Baldegger Lakes, to the East, and the Lake of Sempach, to the West, passing through Munster. This route bisected the Lucernese line of defence. The 2d corps, division-DONATS, advanced upon the 4th road, through Sursee, along the western shore of the Lake of Sempach and in sight of the battle fields of Buttisholz and Sempach, both so glorious to the republican Swiss; the first as disastrous to the English Free Companies, in 1375, as the second had been to the Austrians, in 1386. The 3d corps, division-BURCKHARDT, directed its march by the 5th and most western road upon Willisau, the extreme left of the Rebels. Meanwhile a 4th corps, reserve-division-OCHSENBEIN, threatened, from the West, the *left*-rear of the Lucernese, just as this force, under his orders, had menaced the right-rear of the Freyburghers. Ochsenbein, at this date a Federal Colonel, became, subsequently, a general in the service of Napoleon III. Having made a rapid return-march through Berne, he was, now, advancing thence, by the difficult, serpentine route through the Emmen-Thal and the Entlibuch. On the 22d November, he had an action at Escholzmatt, on the frontiers of the Canton of Lucerne. On the 23d a more serious engagement, five miles further on, occurred at Schupfheim. Thus advancing slowly and with difficulty, Ochsenbein was forcing his way through, to work in, at the time fixed, as directed, with the rest. This gallant officer now had an opportunity to retrieve the credit he had lost in 1845, by the failure of his aggressive movements on the same road, a failure attributable rather to the indiscipline of his Volunteer troops, (Free Corps) than to any fault of his own. At the same time a sixth column, the brigade-ZELLER, invaded Schwytz through the March, or mountain range, South of the eastern extremity of the Lake of Zurich, converging to take the right flank of the Lucernese line in reverse. A seventh column, the division GMUR, advanced through the bailiwick of Knonau, about two miles west from CAPPEL, where the magnanimous Zwingli, the First of the Great Reformers, was murdered in cold blood, after the battle of the 11th of October, 1531, in which he had been present as Chaplain. He was killed, by a

Roman-Catholic Captain of Unterwalden, while lying wounded and speechless on the field. In like manner, the Romanist Captain of the Swiss Guards of the Duke of Anjou, afterwards Henry III of France, assassinated the Prince of Conde after the battle of Jarnac, 12th or 13th March 1569. The Prince had surrendered and was sitting, exhausted, propped against a tree, with his thigh bone fractured and protruding. when his murderer galloped up and shot him through the head. The same spirit had prompted the Slaughter of the Free Corps and animated many partisans of the Sonderbund. This distribution of the Federal forces is founded on a comparison of the language of Zschokke and Richon, the historians at hand, who present the most detailed accounts of the military movements.

Dufour intended to distract the enemy's attention by these seven distinct menaces and deceive them as to the point on which his real attack was directed. His superiority of force doubtless justified this disposition, although his different divisions and columns were divided from each other by huge mountains, dangerous defiles, broad lakes and rapid streams. He knew that the Rebels would have the greatest difficulty in reinforcing a weak point even if they attempted to do so, while their whole line was equally endangered. Having thus divided the attention of the Rebel leaders and attracted it to so many different quarters, he rapidly massed the bulk of his troops in the point of the Freiamt, shut in between the river Reuss, on the East, and the high range of the Linderberg, to the west. About ten miles north-east of Lucerne, these come together. This acute triangle has a base only five miles wide at Muri, ten miles north of Klein-Dietwyl, half a mile from its apex. A little less than a mile beyond this point, the road crossed the Reuss by a covered bridge, whose issue on the south shore was swept by the heavy artillery of a strong bridge-head. Here the road coming in from the N. E., from Brugg, and the lake of Zug, joined the route from Muri and continued on, through Roth or Root, to Lucerne. Both ran under the fortified heights of the Rothenberg, and, opposite the fork, stood the village of GISLIKON, covered by extensive field works. These strong intrenchments had been finished several months previous, despite the summons of the Federal Diet to stop their construction. Since their completion, the Rebels had guaranteed their possession by constantly maintaining strong garrisons therein. Gislikon had thus become the key to Lucerne on the North. The Lake of the Forest Cantons precluded attack from the South or immediate rear.

On the afternoon of the 22d of November, the confined funnel or triangle between Muri and Dietwyl, above described, was literally gorged or overflowing with troops, destined to make the grand attack. Forward they must when the order to advance was given. The impulsion from the rear would have forced on those in front if their enthusiasm had failed. Momentum would have lent its immense forces to mass. This proved emphatically so, for the leading battalions carried the Rebel works with a rush. Just as FREDERIC stormed the heights of Lissa in 1757; just as LAUDOHN escaladed the ramparts of Schweidnitz in 1761; just as WAYNE charged bayonet into Stony Point in 1779; just as SUWARROW captured Ismail by assault in 1790, and Praga in 1794 ; and just as the French columns, in the narrow streets of Paris, charged over the insurgent barricades, in 1848 and 1851 -- their front ranks carried over, dead or alive, by the accelerated pressure of those behind—just so the Federals poured into the Rebel intrenchments on the ensuing day. This we shall see but more in detail.

During the night of the 22d and 23d November, the Federals threw two bridges of boats across the Reuss, one below the ruins of the permanent structure at Sins, three miles North of Dietwyl, which had been destroyed by the Sonderbundists, the other above the covered bridge of Gislikon. Early on the morning of the 23d, the sub-division EGLOFF crossed by the lower pontoon bridge to turn the Rothenberg from the side of Zug. This manœuvre against the extreme Rebel right, brought on a sharp and protracted conflict which lasted throughout the day. The sub-divisions under Brigadiers ISLER and RITTER, sweeping round to take the enemy's right in reverse, encountered the Rebels advantageously posted on sheltered, rising ground, in the vicinity of Meyers-kappel. The defenders were chiefly Riflemen from the Forest Cantons, armed with weapons to whose use they had been accustomed since their.childhood. After a hot conflict, these were compelled to abandon their position. They retreated, fighting however, behind Udligenschwyl to the Kiemenberg. Here they formed again in order of battle and, again, were driven back, disputing every inch of ground to Ebikon, three miles north ot Lucerne. This was between 2 and 3 P. M. when they were abandoned by their artillery, which galloped off into the invested town. Thus deserted and having to depend upon their rifles alone, the Unterwalden Battalion still held Ebikon after Lucerne itself had surrendered. Entirely forgotten by their generals, the Rebel authorities, in fact by their whole party, they still presented an undaunted front when their superiors had fled and all the other troops had submitted. All honor to these brave mountain men although fighting in the defence of erroneous principles and obsolete ideas.

Before nightfall, despite the desperate resistance they had encountered, the Federals had thus fought their way to the summit of the Kiemenberg, in the rear of Gislikon. These heights, so gallantly won, commanded the main rebel fortifications, upon which so much skill and labor had been expended in vain. Here the victors bivouaced within six miles, to the N. E., of Lucerne.

Meanwhile the sub-division-EGLOFF stormed the heights in the rear of Honau, after the Zurich artillery had silenced the rebel guns in that position. Driving the enemy before them, they crowned a second summit which commanded Gislikon. Here the two sub-divisions ZIEGLER and EGLOFF were to have effected a junction, and, thence, to have moved, simultaneously, against the principal defences of the Sonderbundists. This junction did not take place. Ziegler's division had passed the Reuss later on the 23d, by the upper bridge of boats, above Gislikon, to attack the north side of the Rothenberg. These troops, however, had a mighty task before them, and were correspondingly delayed. They had not only to face the heavy artillery in the works enfilading the debouches of the covered bridge of Gislikon, but also those around the village itself. Besides this, the heights of Gislikon were traversed by trenches lined with the practiced riflemen of Unterwalden, and the ridges of the mountain were occupied by militia, accustomed to the use of fire-arms and completely sheltered from their assailants, in the woods.

Finally, amid shouts which must have been heard in Lucerne, the heights and defences of GISLIKON were car-

ried and the loyal artillery of Soleure established there.
The rebel Commander-in-Chief, however inferior to Dufour
in Strategy, was not wanting to himself, in energy, at this
crisis. He headed the rebel troops and made such a desperate counter-attack upon the successful Federals that
they were forced to give ground. Fortunately this part
of the field admitted the rapid manœuvring of artillery.
A Bernese 12-pdr. howitzer battery was brought up at full
gallop and poured a storm of shell upon the opposing
guns. It is claimed that out of sixty shots fired, fifty
hit the points aimed at. They exploded the ammunition
boxes of the rebel artillery, and dispersed the cannoneers
in an instant. Salis-Soglio himself was wounded by the
fragment of a shell. Everything was thrown into ir-
remediable confusion. This artillery charge, improvised
by Colonel DENZLER of Zurich, like the Dragoon charge
made by the younger Kellerman, or the Artillery volley
of Marmont at Marengo, decided the fate of the day. It
was now 4 P. M. Among the Rebels all was terror and
confusion. The fortifications of Gislikon were abandoned;
the militia had already fled from their coverts. There
was fighting on the heights however until night-fall.—
But as darkness closed in the horizon towards the north-
east and north was all aglow with the bivouac-fires of the
victors. To the west likewise, the sky was illuminated,
for, while the principal fighting had been going on so
fiercely towards the north, Ochsenbein's leading battalions
had occupied the plateau and heights of Littan, within
three miles of Lucerne. The city was completely at the
mercy of Dufour. He demanded an unconditional surrender, and the haughty Charleston of the Sonderbund was
forced to throw itself upon the mercy of the Federal Chief.
Thus Dufour, who had smothered the fire of rebellion in
Freyburg in five days, in seven more days quenched

this furnace of revolt. The next morning, the 24th November, an apparently almost endless procession of victorious Unionists poured into the city. To the corps which
had so distinguished themselves upon the Rothenberg, and
those which had fought their way, step by step, for twenty
five miles, through the upper Entlibach, were now united
the Brigade, or Division, Gmur, which had crossed the
Canton of Schwytz, thro the March, and the third division,
whose unopposed advance, through the valley of Hitzkirch,
had been a mere military promenade. Such a magnificent spectacle had never before been witnessed in the
Confederation; 60,000 citizen-soldiery perfectly organized
with all their material and equipages, swelled the triumphant procession of Loyalty through the streets of the Rebel
city. With the troops returned the crowds of proscribed
Unionists, who had been exiled on account of their reformed faith and liberal opinions. Every generous heart
will sympathize with their joy and glory in such a restoration to their native seats.

Previous, however, to the surrender of Lucerne, and
while Salis-Soglio still held out hopes of being able to
maintain his ground at Ebikon, the Jesuits who had been
the moving cause of all the bloodshed, the expenditure,
the losses, and the misery consequent on the Separate
League, the Sonderbund Council of War, the prominent
factious, and even associations of monks and nuns, fled
from the town. These embarked, under the protection
of a company of infantry, on board of a steamboat already
prepared. Twenty land-jagers served as a guard to the
fugitives. They carried with them the treasure and seals
of the State, the archives of the Rebel Council of War,
important official documents, the booty captured by the
foray into the Canton of Ticino, and stores of grain. Thus
they escaped into mountains, and thence into foreign

countries, leaving rich individuals, who had fostered, and wealthy institutions, which had favored, the rebellion, to pay dearly for their wicked co-operation with treason. This may prefigure the fate of our Secession Leaders and Abettors. Like the leading Swiss traitors they may save their worthless lives to expiate in exile and poverty or contumely, amid the hatred and execrations of their dupes, the evil and sorrow they have brought home to the firesides of our common country.

On the 25th, the Cantons of URI, SCHWYTZ and UNTERWALDEN, belonging to the Sonderbund (corresponding to Alabama, Mississippi and Florida in this country), which, in 1798, displayed so much heroism against the French, imitated the prudence of the people of Freyburg, and of Lucerne, and capitulated.

Here we should observe a fact extremely pertinent to our own situation. Notwithstanding the extreme defensibleness of the mountains of Switzerland,—particularly those of the original Forest Cantons, embraced within the limits of the Sonderbund,—as soon as LUCERNE had yielded, the Rebel Leaders, at once, acknowledged that the fate of Swiss Secession depended upon the possession of the large fortified towns, and upon the maintenance of the armies massed in and about them. This should be a consolation to those who fear that a GUERILLA WAR in the South can lead to any successful result or defer, for more than a short period, its entire subjugation. The Sonderbund Generals saw at a glance the game was up, after their armies had been dissipated and the principal places taken. So it will be with our Southern Secession. It will collapse at once when the armies of LEE, BRAGG, BEAUREGARD, JOHNSON and MAGRUDER are destroyed.

On the 29th November, the VALAIS,—beyond the lofty

Bernese Alps and along the Rhone,—which might be said to represent the Rebel territory beyond the Mississippi,—the Texas and most remote border State of Switzerland, the focus of retrograde ideas, bordering on the most bigoted district of Sardinia, petitioned to be received back into the Union.

Meanwhile on the 27th November, 23 days after the decree of the Diet or Congress, had ordered the Swiss General to draw his sword and unfurl the Federal standard, the military chief of the Union was enabled to announce that the Secession Alliance was dissolved. The fire-eating Cantons had gained nothing by their rashness but the humiliating conviction of their own weakness as compared with the Federal power and will.*

Let Traitors and Demagogues, whom the thirst for power induces to pander to spiritual and material despotism, read a lesson in the fate of the Swiss Sonderbund, Separate or Secession League, and its Leaders. "That (Separate League) which had been proclaimed before Europe as the rock of religion and of true freedom, collapsed at the first dash of the waves like a house built upon the sand." It is to be hoped that the Cotton-States-Confederate-League, built upon the corner stone of Slavery, will likewise utterly perish between the shattering of war and the earthquake of moral regeneration. The spiritual guides (not inaptly reproduced in our own country by the slavocrat divines) who had excited their dupes to rebellion in Switzerland by pretended miracles, had not inspired them with the same resolution, to maintain the

* It is but just to myself to state that an Article entitled "SECESSION IN SWITZERLAND" was furnished by me, in February, 1861, to the New York Evening Post, and published in the first column, first page, of that paper. If the example which the Swiss Authorities presented for our instruction, had been imitated by our Government, this War would not have been dragged on through fearful years. Nevertheless the Delay has been Providential, for it has effectually solved the Problem, whether Slavery or the Union shall survive, and proved that Slavery is incompatible with Free Institutions. Now that Slavery is doomed, if we are faithful to God and true to ourselves, what a glorious Career looms up before our Nation in the Future.   J. W. DE P.

Independence of the Separate League, that their real
wrongs and a good cause had given them to win and
maintain the freedom of the same districts, centuries
before and against greater odds. " The Jesuits had
everywhere fled on the entrance of the Confederates,"
says Zschokke, "now they were forever banished from
Swiss soil." The rebellion had been so promptly extinguished that the French envoy actually had not time
to proffer foreign assistance, or even to propose to mediate
between the Federal Diet and the Council of War of the
Seven Rebel Cantons. Its members were already fugitives when the French messenger went to seek them. At
the outbreak of hostilities the French ministers with other
Diplomatists had retired to neutral or, as we would term
it, " copperhead " or "peace-party" NEUCHATEL. That
Canton and another, INNER-APPENZELL, which had refused to perform their duty as loyal Confederates during
the war, were subjected to very heavy fines for the benefit
of the reorganized Confederation.

Nor were the Expulsion of the Jesuits and the pecuniary suffer-
ings of the Neutral Sonderbund, the only consequences of this mad
attempt " to arrest the effulgent chariot of Holy Liberty." "Lucerne," temporarily ruined, " instituted judicial suits against the
members of her former council for embezzlement of the public
money, and confiscated the estates of those who provoked the war."
" Shortly afterwards she sought a doubtful remedy by suppressing
the convents, that she might be indemnified by their property ; and
the people before whose veto the decree was laid, did not refuse
their consent." The members of the Freyburg Council who had
voted for the Separate League " were brought to a most severe
account in discharging the war expenses." " The Valais, also, laid
almost all her share of the expenses upon those who had voted for,
advised and preached the war." These burthens had to be especially borne by the monastical and other ecclesiastical institutions
which had hoped to profit by the rebellion. In fact the Sonderbund Cantons were called upon to reimburse the War Expenses
incurred by the Confederacy. They were militarily occupied until
the first installment had been paid and adequate security given for
the balance. " Great reforms now took place (in 1848) in all the
Cantons of the former Sonderbund. *Even in* URI, *where, since*
TELL's *time, no written constitution had ever existed, one was now
drawn up and accepted* by the communes."

No Failure could have been more decided, no Sup-

pression more mortifying than that of the Ultramontane
or Secession League in Switzerland. No Action could
have been more prompt and energetic, no Triumph more
complete and beneficial than that of the Swiss Loyalists
or Union party.

"One cannot too much admire the calm firmness which the men
who presided over the destinies of the Confederation manifested in
1847. Menaced by France, Russia, Prussia, and Austria, and having
at their disposal only a portion of the forces of a nation which does
not possess altogether two millions and a half of citizens, they were
discouraged neither by the intrigues of the monks, nor by the
anathemas of the Romish clergy; by the anger of certain empirics,
nor by the military reputation of those Cantons, which were so
sadly misled by fatal influences. What an example for such countries as are wont to be alarmed on account of their comparative
weakness ! *Switzerland has taught them that a people, conscious of
its right, and resolved to defend it, has nothing to fear on earth."*

This Triumph of Patriotism realized the Truth of
Zschokke's prophetic declaration, that *"Heaven helps only
those who march joyously to battle and to death in a just
cause; but rejects those who sit sluggishly in arrogant
security."*

Eighteen days of military operations, which might even
be reduced to fifteen of manœuvring and fighting, anni-
hilated the Sonderbund. The history of the world presents but few examples of such a speedy solution of a
great political problem. The most pertinent examples
are the destruction, in a few days, of the Bohemian Kingdom of the Elector-Palatine, Frederic, by the generals of
Ferdinand II; the total defeat of the Belgian armies,
in eight days, by the heroic Prince of Orange, and
the complete overthrow, in three days, of the Sardinian
armaments by Radetsky. Compared however with the
rout of the Weissen-Berg, in 1620, the conflicts of Has-
selt in 1830, and the battle of Novara, in 1849, the
combat of Gislikon, in 1847, was a mere fiasco. "A
whiff of grape-shot," to use a Napoleonic expression, or,
more properly speaking, a flurry of shells, blew away the
pretentions of the Sonderbund.

The final result seems to justify the idea that the madness and incipient success of the Separate League was permitted by Providence, in order that its suppression might convince Switzerland of the defects of its *dislocated* Confederacy, and induce the Cantons to consent to a more determined Centralization of authority.

The Separate League which was to have divided Switzerland; to have arrested the progress of the age; to have restored abuses for the benefit of the few to the suffering of the many; had a directly opposite result. It transmuted the loose Confederation of XXII Independent Cantons into a well-knit Nationality of twenty two members.

May the example not be lost upon us. May Providence conduct our affairs to the same happy result that he vouchsafed in the case of the Swiss, must be the prayer of every honest man and true patriot.

The lessons of this history we think can scarcely be lost upon us. The effort to shatter the ALPINE REPUBLIC, in a brief period, proved a miserable failure, and the attempt here made to divide and destroy our Free Government, we know will, in God's good time, come to naught. And even as the National Life Struggle, in Switzerland, ended in a more healthy and vigorous NATIONAL EXISTENCE, so, we trust, that the fiery trial through which we as a people are now passing, will eventuate not only in a restored UNITY, but, if need be, in a STRONGER DEMOCRATIC-REPUBLICAN GOVERNMENT, better fitted to perform its great work, and hold its commanding position among the Nations.

"God of our Fathers, hear our earnest Cry!
Our Hope, our Strength, our Refuge is in Thee.
Confound our Foes, and make their Legions fly;
Strengthen our Hosts and give them Victory!
Victory!—Victory!—
Oh, God of Armies, give us Victory!"

"For the sad Millions of the groaning Earth,
Helpless and crushed beneath Oppression's Rod,
For every Hope that hallows Home and Hearth,
For heaven-born Liberty, the Child of God,
Victory!—Victory!—
God of the Nations, give us Victory!

"From War's red Hell, involved in smoke and flame,
From up-piled Altars of our noblest Dead,
We cry to Thee! oh, for Thy glorious Name,
Make bare Thine Arm and smite our Foes with dread,
VICTORY!—VICTORY!—
OH, GOD OF BATTLES, GIVE US VICTORY!"

ANCEOR

www.ingramcontent.com/pod-product-compliance
Lightning Source LLC
Chambersburg PA
CBHW020251090426
42735CB00010B/1884

* 9 7 8 3 3 3 7 1 5 3 7 4 8 *